Finding the
Right Woman
for You

michelle mckinney hammond

HARVEST HOUSE PUBLISHERS

EUGENE, OREGON

Cover by Koechel Peterson & Associates, Inc., Minneapolis, Minnesota

FINDING THE RIGHT WOMAN FOR YOU
Copyright © 2005 by Michelle McKinney Hammond
Published by Harvest House Publishers
Eugene, Oregon 97402
www.harvesthousepublishers.com

Library of Congress Cataloging-in-Publication Data

McKinney Hammond, Michelle, 1957-
    Finding the right woman for you / Michelle McKinney Hammond
p. cm.
    ISBN 0-7369-1506-0 (pbk.)
    1. Bible. O.T. Ruth—Criticism, interpretation, etc. 2. Mate selection—Religious aspects—Christianity. I. Title
BS1315.52.M34 2004
241'.6765—dc22   2004015771

Printed in the United States of America.

05 06 07 08 09 10 11 12 / VP-CF / 10 9 8 7 6 5 4 3 2 1

Contents

Attention, Please...

*M*en, it is time for us to have a talk, to get real: man to woman, woman to man. Rumor has it, according to the men, a good woman is hard to find, even though there are many women available in assorted shapes, sizes, and colors. Finding a *really* good one seems to be an impossible proposition. Now for the inside scoop: The women are saying the same thing about you! Truly, it is time to get matters of the heart in perspective and lay sound ground rules for finding and keeping the love you want. This might seem impossible to you, but there is hope. For men and women, finding "The One" seems to be as elusive as finding a needle in a haystack. Perhaps your own mind-set could be hindering your search. What you are looking for could be standing right in front of you, but you have failed to recognize her. This is what I would like to address in my time with you. As a sister trying to help a brother out, I am going to give you the 4-1-1 on women and how to recognize a really good one. After that, the rest will be up to you.

5

Before we begin, I want to paint the picture of what most women typically see when they go out, and perhaps why the good ones have gone into hiding. I want to examine why our mating instincts have become confused, before I delve into what to do about it. Bear with me and see if this scenario is not a familiar one to you.

Several evenings ago, before leaving for a road trip, a friend and I decided to grab a quick dinner at a restaurant in my neighborhood that had just opened. Though it was early, we were told that the dining room was full. If we liked, we could be seated in the lounge and order from the menu there. We were then escorted to the lower level of the restaurant, and greeted by pulsating music and a dreamlike atmosphere. Couples, female clusters, male partners, and mixed groups of friends were lounging and reclining, languidly gazing around the room, or caught up in animated conversation.

The men were looking, the women were strutting, but no one was connecting. Now this leads to a whole discussion on its own. What has happened to men? Why don't they talk to women? Where has the hunter instinct gone? We will discuss this in a later chapter. To be perfectly honest, I felt a bit naïve. I had left this sort of scene so long ago that the subtleties of it were no longer clear to me. I had vague remembrances of my B.C. days (before establishing a relationship with Christ), of hanging out, meeting guys at the bar or on the dance floor, and having brief flings that never went anywhere. After all, how seriously could you take someone you had met under these circumstances? This could explain why you will not find what you are looking for in these types of places.

There always seemed to be a cloud of suspicion hanging over these newfound dates. Where had they come from? Were they seeing anyone else? Who were their friends? What was their background? Who were they really? Were they always on the prowl? Had fate actually worked in your favor on that chance encounter? Too many questions and uncertainties usually clouded any potential for true love with trust issues before two people could even get started.

That night it seemed nothing had changed, except that men were much bolder years ago. They clocked the woman they wanted and moved in for the kill, because everyone understood that was what we were all out for. This new scene of people passing one another in a solo dance that was designed for two was troubling at best.

"What was the point?" my friend and I asked. Here were all these women dressed to the nines, I mean *really* dressed to impress: backless, strapless, short short, spike heels, flawless makeup...and not a bite. They got lots of stares, but no takers. I wondered, as we left, if anyone made a love connection before the evening was over, and how many people went home disappointed that once again their search for love had turned up empty. How many women wondered if they should have gone up and introduced themselves or been more aggressive or worn a different outfit? How many men kicked themselves for not saying "hello"? How many men wondered if the woman who caught their eye was as nice as she seemed? Would they see her again and have a second chance to find out?

How ironic that in a world where everyone longs for the same thing, true love remains elusive for many people. If everyone is searching for love, why is it so hard for us to find one another? That mystery question will be answered when someone finally figures out why traffic is backed up if all the cars are moving on a highway. It is one of the great mysteries of life.

Can you find the woman of your dreams? Can the search for love be fruitful? I believe it can be when we plant the right seeds and purposefully apply ourselves to giving the love we want to find. Because love is not just a feeling but a decision, the head must work with the heart to make intelligent choices that lead to love. Chemistry—as well as charm and beauty—can be deceitful, so even though it is needed in the mix, it cannot be all there is. As we take a look at an ancient account of a man who found lasting love in the most unexpected place, we will dissect the Bible story of Ruth and Boaz to find principles that can be applied to your life. But first, I must ask you some questions:

+ Are you really ready for the love you think you want?

+ What is your motivation for desiring a committed love relationship?

+ What problems do you think love will solve in your world (or create)?

+ What are you prepared to give in order to get the love you desire?

+ Do you know what you want in a woman? Are your expectations realistic?

+ If you never found Ms. Right, would you still be able to lead a happy and fulfilled life?

These questions might take some time and deep thought for you to answer, but certain heart issues must be settled before we even begin. I understand that men have many fears and suspicions when it comes to women, as well as many insecurities about themselves. First, one of the great barriers to finding lasting love is being out of touch with who you are and what you really need. The second barrier is the inability of both sexes to understand each other. Women expect men to think like women, and men just do not know what women are thinking. Period! Perhaps as I let you know what women really need from you, it will help some of your imaginary insufficiencies to be dispersed and empower you to step up to the plate and claim your bride.

This book is just as much about you as it is about women. I will tell you how to find the woman you want and need, as well as how to capture her heart. Notice I said *you* will find *her*. It is the job of a *real* man to find his woman, pursue her, and capture her heart. I realize roles have gotten confused in recent years and women have become more aggressive, but it is up to a man to reclaim his masculinity and set his relationships back in the right spiritual order. This will only occur if you have your head and your heart together. So let's begin. It is time to settle outstanding issues to which you might not have given much thought, preparing yourself to love and to be loved in return.

1
Love Hunger

In the days when the judges ruled,
there was a famine in the land....

RUTH 1:1

*S*o begins the story of hunger, longing, unfulfillment, and even starvation. Surveys say that men date more often than women. Why? Because there are more available women than men, and women have to wait to be asked, for the most part. Though some men do not, it is probably safe to say that, in most instances, if the man does not do the choosing, the bold woman becomes someone to occupy his time until he finds a woman he really wants to pursue. Now that we have agreed on that, let's be honest. Are you really any more fulfilled from dating several women whom you instinctively know are not "The One" until you find her? It actually heightens your state of disgruntlement, doesn't it? Because men were created and programmed for bonding with a special woman, the hunger remains. Do not fight the feeling. It is only natural. To love and be loved by that one woman who will rock your world and complete you is a drive hidden deep in the heart of every man who is yielded to God's design for his life (unless he has been called to be a monk, of course. Because you bought this book, I assume this would not apply to you.)

Turn on your television any day of the week and it is clearly evident that when it comes to the search for love, we are in a state of emergency. The plethora of matchmaking stunts reveals the urgency of men and women, no matter what race or class, to try to find true love at all costs, even being willing to embarrass themselves on a national scale to compete for the attention of a bachelorette or bachelor. The looks of disappointment and the level of frustration displayed after not being chosen *by a stranger* tell the tale. People are desperate. Men and women feel their options for finding a lasting, committed relationship are quickly vanishing, along with their hopes to fulfill their deepest longing: to love and be loved.

The hunger for love can do strange things to a man. It can cause him to become distracted in his life mission. There is a sense of not being clearly defined because of the boundaries that come with being accountable to and responsible for another human being. A lack of grounding and permanence can cause a man to second-guess his career choices and passions. He finds it hard to settle into a mode of productive living or complete projects and tasks. There is a sense of being a nomad that pervades every area of his life, from physical living conditions to the way he handles jobs and relationships.

This is normal. God made a man to be completed by a woman who will help define him and the choices he makes in life. The very first man, Adam, set the blueprint in place. God decided after giving Adam his assignment in life—to be fruitful and multiply, to practice authority over everything that was placed under his power, to take dominion over his environment and circumstances—that he would need a partner to accomplish this overwhelming charge. With this in mind, God created woman to be his able partner, designed and suited specifically for him. She would balance him and be strong where he was weak. Her special gifts and sensitivities would complete the big picture of effectual daily living. Together, they would be a powerful team, able to master life between them.

There are a lot of successful single men, so how does this fit the picture of a man needing a woman to help him? If a man is passionate enough about his craft and reaches a place where he has experienced a degree of success, the clock in his head says he should have a family to accompany his success. This leads him on a frenzied search for something that will put out the fire of yearning that nestles deep within his soul. Unfortunately, this hunger leads to the wrong places, in a lot of circumstances. This is where the games begin.

The games run the gamut from seasons of deep self-involvement that include unproductive, self-defeating, unhealthy habits, to a string of unfulfilling and damaging relationships with members of the opposite sex. Many a moment is spent pondering the resounding question, "Where have all the good women gone?" The answer appears more and more elusive as resolutions are drawn that it is not necessary to be married when there is a world of women out there to keep a man distracted. Hunger ignored simply burrows deeper into the inner recesses of the heart and manifests itself in other ways. The problem with love hunger is that it is real. How we feed it has an effect on our health—physically, emotionally, and spiritually.

When we are hungry physically, and we are not in the position to have a balanced, healthy meal, we have a tendency to settle for junk food. We choose empty calories or something that is filling but also fattening, seemingly satisfying but not nutritious. When we are hungry emotionally, we can make choices that are just as unhealthy. We have a tendency to settle for what is available: empty, no-win relationships with people that we know are not good for us, who could never be prospects for a committed relationship. Many times we will emerge from these relationships with more baggage, more disabling deadweight, and an even deeper hunger from all the negative experiences we have endured for the sake of having an "affirming moment" here and there.

No one should crucify himself for wanting love. The longing for love is a natural human emotion. It is a spiritual instinct, built into the center of our souls by the Author of love Himself: God. God also longs for love from all of His creation. He placed this hunger in our hearts to cause us to reach first for Him, and secondly for one another. We should desire to love and be loved. But the desire for love should not rule us to the point where we look for it in all the wrong places, trying to fulfill our longing with unhealthy alternatives, or becoming paralyzed by our yearning.

It is not a good idea to go grocery shopping or order a meal at a restaurant when we are hungry. When our eyes are bigger than our stomachs, we have a tendency to make bad choices or overdo the amount of food we order, and end up with things we do not need and cannot finish. Everything looks good when we are hungry. We will pay a high price for hunger that is out of control. At the end of the day, we still will not be satisfied. Those men who have settled for *something* rather than having *nothing* in the area of relationships have found themselves more miserable than when they were alone.

How did our hunger become so overwhelming if it is a God-given instinct? We might say that from the moment our mother Eve and her husband, Adam, shared a bite out of the forbidden fruit in the garden, we all inherited the consequences of their little afternoon snack. The punishment for deciding God was not enough to fulfill all of their desires landed them in a place where their appetites would never be satisfied. The woman's desire for validation and affirmation from her man would put undue pressure on men for generations to come as they struggle to fill the spot in a woman's heart they were never designed to fill. Man would also struggle with his identity as he strove to produce a life through his work that validated his masculinity and proved to his woman he was worthy of her respect.

The misconception that, apart from his achievements, a man would not be worthy of a woman's love became a lie planted in man's spirit on that fateful afternoon. This deception would cause difficulties between men and women up to present day. Man spends a lifetime trying to measure up to a woman's expectations. Meanwhile, he has formed a few of his own expectations about what a woman should look like and how his relationship with her is supposed to affect him. Today, false expectations of how the other person is supposed to make us feel cause us to pass up many a likely candidate for life partner because we keep looking for something or someone to fill the spot that only God can fill.

You see, God has reserved a spot in your heart for Himself. Once He is allowed to sit on the throne of your heart, you will find all of your deepest desires fulfilled by Him. The right woman will just be the icing on the cake of your life. Your identity and the definition of who you are will be fulfilled by the One who has created you and loved you most. However, if you decide to cancel His reservation and become "independent," to "make your own choices," and to allow something else to become more important than your connection to Him, your hunger will only increase. Be it your career, the state of your muscles, your material acquisitions, or a woman in your life, once you decide to launch into the deep of your own desires, you will find yourself hungrier than ever.

So how do we handle love hunger in a healthy manner? I understand, that men's hunger is two-faceted. A woman's desire for love is married to her desire for sexual intimacy, in most instances, whereas men are able to separate the two. The spiritual need for love is pushing men inwardly, while the physical desire for sex is driving them outwardly. This can be overwhelming for a man who is struggling to live by godly principles as a single male. Many men have asked, "If God isn't going to give me the desire of my heart, why won't He take the desire away?" Let me help you out here. He is not going to take away your desire. He gave you that desire. However, He will help you to master your desires if you allow Him to.

"Well, how do I do that, Michelle?" you ask. First of all, deal with the reality of your love hunger. The interesting thing about physical hunger is even though you may feel hunger, the body does not go into starvation mode immediately. The body is able to feed on itself for 40 days before it begins to react negatively to not having food. The first reality about love hunger is you will not die without a woman in your life or without sex. Can you exist and actually thrive instead of just survive? The answer is absolutely yes! I am a witness.

Your love hunger is not bad unless it is controlling you—overtaking your every thought and coloring your decisions. If this is the case, it is time to take back control. First step, get a love life. "Exactly how do I do that?" you ask. "After all, that is why I bought the book!" True, so let's take it one step at a time. I am going to break this down into something you can use. If you are willing to do the work, I promise you that the truth will equip you to make yourself free. Along the way, you will find confessions in call-out boxes. I suggest you hide these confessions in your heart and let them roll around in your head until they become a part of you.

First, feed on the sources of love that God has already placed in your life. That would include God first, then you (yes, you!), and then your neighbors: friends, family, and even others. Yes, this truly can be accomplished. In order to make wise selections that are nutritious to your body, as well as your heart and soul, you must be full and whole already. The full soul will loathe even the honeycomb, but the empty soul will find even a bitter thing sweet. Remember the opening verse to this chapter? It said that when the judges ruled, there was a famine. When your flesh or your emotions rule, you become a prime candidate for a famine of the heart. But when God rules, your heart is fertile ground for joyous fulfillment, regardless of if there is a woman in your life or not.

Your relationship with God sets the stage for how all of your relationships will play out. Remember that the first famous commandment (not suggestion), from our heavenly Creator is: "Love the Lord your God with all your heart, soul, mind, and strength." This is followed by the second commandment that everyone knows, even if the person has never cracked open a Bible: "Love your neighbor as yourself." You cannot love anyone else properly until you love yourself, and you cannot love yourself properly unless you make a love connection with God and have a passionate, intimate relationship with Him.

This might be hard for you to receive. I find that truly manly men have a problem relating to God as the Lover of their souls. I propose this approach: Why not see God as a loving Father and Jesus as the "friend that sticks closer than a brother"? See Jesus as the One who has your back,

Personal Confession

I will no longer allow my hunger to drive me into the arms of women who were not designed to be my partner in life. I will not confuse and hurt any woman because of my desire to fulfill my own needs, but will choose to walk in discipline, redeeming the time until I commit to the one woman that God has for me.

the One who will be there for you through thick and thin—your Jonathan. David, king of Israel, when considering the rich friendship he had with his friend Jonathan, declared that Jonathan's love for him was more wonderful than that of a woman. He was not physically attracted to or involved with Jonathan. What he was referring to was the faithfulness of Jonathan as a friend. Jonathan was the son of his worst enemy, King Saul. Jonathan knew that God was going to take the throne away from his father and give it to David, yet he refused to side with his father in his vendetta against David. Instead,

Jonathan defended David and helped him escape! That is God for you. He will be your Friend, Confidant, and Partner. He will defend you against the enemy and his lies—the lies that can wreak havoc on your self-esteem.

It is important to settle your esteem problems as a man. Why? Because you have the capacity to seriously damage a woman. That damaged woman, in turn, will hurt some other unsuspecting brother, which then ruins him for the next woman. The cycle goes on and on. Get the picture? There are a host of men who pursue women but do not really like women. Subconsciously, the anger and unresolved pain they harbor, from either their relationship with their mother or past relationship with another woman who planted this unhealthy seed in their spirits, causes them to punish women by seducing their hearts and then withholding their own emotions. Thus begins a vicious cat-and-mouse game—the woman trying to help draw this man out while he flip-flops from Dr. Jekyll to Mr. Hyde.

In the end, his coldness and inability to give her the love and tenderness she craves results in her plummeting to the depths of low self-esteem. Only a discerning woman would be able to tell that the problem does not lie with her, but with her charming yet elusive beau. On the other hand, many men suffer with the inability to commit because of fear of rejection and abandonment issues. The relationship becomes "dump or be dumped," lying just beneath the veneer of, "It's a guy thing, you know. We're programmed to conquer as many women as we can." Not in God's kingdom, you don't. Your fears must be addressed and put to rest in order for you to have fulfilling relationships. Unfortunately, the inability to commit will bleed over into more than your relationships with women. It will affect every aspect of your life and hinder you from progressing in an effective manner at work and elsewhere.

Ah...but when we are connected to the original Lover of our souls, we are brimming over with validation and affirmation that liberates us to love freely, commit readily, and honor the commitments we make. In Matthew 4:4, Jesus states, "Man does not live on bread alone, but on every word that comes from the mouth of God." Notice He did not mention other relationships as a means of sustenance. After all, Adam survived and even thrived while walking and talking with God all by himself before Eve was presented to him. He did not even realize he had a need until God brought it up! If this is the case, it stands to reason that we get sustenance from God not only by reading the Bible, but also by our personal interaction with Him through prayer and fellowship. It is during this time we spend with Him, not just talking but also listening, that life-giving words are spoken into our spirit that strengthen, renew, heal, and fill us to overflowing with the assurance of God's faithfulness and goodness. Not only does He give us assurance of His love for us, but He also gives us the keys to living the life we want to lead.

Now that God has our ear, He promises to provide us with a great filler loaded with nutrition for our souls. He will reveal our purpose and how to operate in it. This is crucial to a man's well-being. It defines who he is. Jesus said His nourishment came from doing the will of His Father and finishing the work He had been sent to do. How much more fulfilled do we feel when we lay our heads down at night

Personal Confession

I will allow God to do the work that needs to be done in my heart to make me a whole person before I pursue a love relationship.

knowing we have done what we were created to do? We have used our natural gifts to make a productive and effective contribution to the life of someone who needed what we had to offer.

Our gifts and talents are the things people celebrate about us, but we find to be no big deal. Because the ability comes naturally to us, that is why it is called a gift. Everyone cannot do what we do the *way* we do it. An effectual prayer would be to ask God how to take our natural talents and abilities and capitalize on them to bless other people and prosper ourselves emotionally, spiritually, and perhaps even financially. That overlooked ability we have with fixing things, working with numbers, counseling people, or whatever—we need to use it for the benefit of other people and the glory of God. Then we can stand back, survey our handiwork, and smile because someone benefited from an encounter with us.

With the Source of your fulfillment securely in place, you are then free to have and experience a myriad of relationships that can only enrich your life. This sense of fulfillment becomes the foundation for satisfying exchanges with family members, fruitful experiences with friends, and rich platonic relationships with the women in your life until you find Ms. Right.

I urge you to nurture incredible friendships with women with one word of caution: Always be clear with them. Let them know exactly where they stand in your life and do not send out mixed signals. Now is not the time to collect a string of lonely hearts until you meet the one you are looking for. It is easy for male and female friends to become surrogate mates for one another while you both wait. Resist the temptation to do so. Though you are clear in your mind that you never intend to marry Sally, she may be secretly hoping that you will change your mind. Therefore, remain transparent with her and do not blur the lines just for your own comfort.

This is a friend you will need before and after marriage. There is a lot to learn about women, and who better to learn from than a friend who will answer you honestly and live with transparency before you? The only way this can be achieved is if you are so full of love and life already, that you can take or leave the appetizers that are presented to you and wait for the main entrée.

The Facts on Women

➤ Though a woman may be concerned with finances, she is more moved by romance from a man. A poor man can have any woman he wants if he is rich in love.

➤ Women are just as hungry for love and intimacy as you are, if not more. Remember, the woman was created for the man! It is this built-in need for a man's love that makes them vulnerable to your advances. Think before you pursue.

➤ No woman can ever truly satisfy your craving for love because she was not designed to do so. Your diet must consist of God's love first. Everything else is the icing.

➤ A woman who pursues you in the beginning of the relationship is already running the relationship. She will not submit to you later. Avoid her at all costs. Self-confidence is one thing. Aggressiveness is another.

➤ Women convince themselves that if you do not want them now, there is always the chance you will come around later. Stay clear with your lady friends on exactly where your heart stands toward them— gently, but firmly.

Consider This

- How does your love hunger manifest itself? What have been the consequences?

- Does your lifestyle reflect that of a settled spirit ready for commitment, or of a nomad still seeking roots? What steps do you need to take to be ready for commitment?

- What parts of your life have you neglected while searching for the right woman? What actions can you take right now to accomplish your goals until you find Ms. Right?

◄►

Why spend money on what is not bread,
and your labor on what does not satisfy?
Listen, listen to me, and eat what is good,
and your soul will delight in the
richest of fare (Isaiah 55:2).

2

The Land of Do-It-Yourself

*And a certain man of Bethlehem, Judah, went to dwell
in the country of Moab...and remained there....
Then Elimelech, Naomi's husband died.*

RUTH 1:1-3 NKJV

*W*henever we allow our love hunger to rule over us, we begin to look for love in all the wrong places. Love hunger is not relegated just to singles. The story tells us that a married couple, as well as two single young men, left the safe haven of Bethlehem (which means "house of bread") in Judah (which means "praise"), and went to a place called Moab. You see, if we do not know our purpose, why we are where we are, we will become distracted by our hunger, fail to realize that all we need is already right where we are, and we will move from the place where God has placed us in order to receive our heart's desire.

The man leading this expedition from the house of bread was Elimelech, which means "God is my King." Amazingly, when we are overwhelmed by hunger, we forget who we are, who God is, and how He is able to supply all of our needs. We step out of character and do things that go against the grain of who we were created to be: people who trust God and His timing for our lives. Judah may be a physical place, but praise is a state of the mind and heart. Nurturing a thankful spirit in spite of what we hunger for will feed our soul faster than allowing discontent to ravage us. Discontent will always lead us astray and straight into the Land of "Do-It-Yourself." That is exactly what Moab (meaning "child of her father") represents. Doing it yourself is exactly where the enemy of your soul, the enemy of your joy, wants you. When you choose to do things yourself, or take life into your own hands, you will always end up with more than you bargained for, which adds up to nothing good.

Let's consider how Moab came to be. After Lot fled from Sodom and Gomorrah with his two daughters, they stopped to lodge in the side of a mountain. As the two daughters considered their fate and what it meant for the future, the alarm on their biological clocks sounded. The two sisters fretted because they now had no husbands and were in danger of not being able to have children. They concocted a scheme to get their father drunk and sleep with him in order to become impregnated. The two sons that they bore were named Ben-Ammi and Moab. The two sons grew into nations that were terrible enemies of Israel—the Ammonites and the Moabites. Because of these nations' incestuous beginning, they inherited a nature that was distasteful to God: worshiping idols, having orgies, indulging in lascivious behavior...you name it.

Moab went a step further. The king of Moab hired the prophet Balaam to curse the nation of Israel on their way to the Promised Land. When this strategy did not work, the women of Moab did a fine job of using their sensual wiles to distract and seduce the men of Israel. They literally led them into idol worship. Because of this, God declared Moabites to be enemies, and they were not allowed to enter into the assembly of the Lord. The Israelites were not to even seek the peace and prosperity of the Moabites, and that was the end of that. Moabites were to be avoided at all cost. Moab was considered enemy territory. Nothing good could possibly come out of Moab.

Now there are a few things we need to consider here. The story goes that Elimelech and his family remained in Moab! I am sure after they got to Moab and considered the customs that were so foreign to their own, they had to question their choice. Did they really want their sons Mahlon (which means "sickly") and Chilion (which means "wasting away") to live in this society and assimilate to these people's habits that they knew were not pleasing to God? By their names we know that they were already susceptible to sickness and death. Their new environment could be detrimental, yet this couple's hunger told them they had no choice, and Mahlon and Chilion obviously did not protest their decision.

Personal Confession

I will resist the urge to lean on my own understanding and will rely on the voice of God for direction in the major decisions of my life. I will consider and heed His instruction in spite of how I feel and what I intellectually reason.

Many of us are this way. We know that we should not remain in the situation we are in, yet we stay in a dead-end relationship because something feels better than nothing. However, the price we pay is dear. Eventually the relationship comes to an end because God will not suffer it to continue. In the aftermath, we are assaulted by rejection and the realization of wasted time, emotions, and energy we will never be able to retrieve. If you fell into sexual sin, a piece of your soul was left with that woman, and you can never regain it. And the void she left behind will follow you into your next relationship. After too many of these repeat performances, you are simply an empty shell with nothing left to give except mistrust should the right woman come along.

It is important to your emotional well-being and health that you make an honest assessment of your situation. Is it conducive to you having the life and fulfillment you so deeply desire? Or are you merely slapping a Band-Aid over an untended wound, hoping you will feel better? We know if we do not deal with cuts properly, they can fester and infect our entire body. There is no bandage that can cover an empty or hurting heart. It must be brought to light, cleansed, and healed with time and the right attention. Loneliness must be put into perspective. You are greater than the feeling. Stop and take stock. It is a feeling that eventually passes. Though it may revisit you often, it does pass! Have a strategy for what you will do when loneliness visits. One strategy should be to not get involved in unfruitful relationships or those that bear the wrong kind of fruit. Do not compromise your morals and standards because a feeling says you should.

Personal Confession

I will not allow myself to remain in situations that are not fruitful or contributing to my well-being physically, emotionally, or spiritually.

Feed your love hunger with things that build you up and make you a better you, from digging into the Word of God to activities that stimulate, invigorate, and fulfill you. Focus on relationships and friendships that nurture and build you up. Actually, this is a great time to assess what you want out of life and get busy making those things happen. I will share more on this later. The bottom line is we can waste away without realizing it when we stay in the wrong place, the wrong situation, the wrong relationships.

The Biological-Clock Issue

Now is the time to discuss a matter men do not usually think about until they are caught in the middle of this life-altering situation. A man needs to be aware of the biological-clock issue and how it can affect him for the rest of his life. If this is not the case for abstinence, I do not know what is. Many women, after reaching a certain age, begin to consider how many years of good childbearing time they have left. If you happen to be the lucky candidate in their lives when this occurs, you could be in trouble. I am addressing this because, unfortunately, there are many Christians who do not practice celibacy. Single mothers have become just as big an issue in the church as out of it. This could not happen unless the men cooperated.

Many single women operate with this mind-set. The moment you begin discussing a future with this wonderful woman, the fact that you would love to have children with her, many women feel they have permission to throw precaution to the wind and get started on that family, even though you are not married. Because most men leave birth control up to the woman, they find themselves shocked to receive the announcement that they are to become the proud father of a child they had not planned. Not only that, but this same woman now expects you to move forward with marriage plans. After all, had you not already discussed them? Sometimes, even if you did not discuss future hopes and dreams with her, she has decided you would be as good a father as any to give her the child she wants. She might discard you after that. She might want your financial support but not your presence, or she may want nothing at all. Yes, men, some women do plot and plan to have your children! You play into their hands when you give in to your flesh outside the safe confines of marriage.

Now let's talk about you. You end up feeling trapped. And well you should, because you are. You will be expected to care for this child, as well as the woman. Because you feel trapped, your first instinct is to flee. The more you try to extricate yourself from the relationship, the angrier she will become. And you know what they say about a spurned woman—she becomes vengeful. Even the sweetest Christian woman can show you an entirely different side of her character when operating under the pressure of this difficult situation.

If you decide to marry her, you will harbor anger for being forced into a decision before you were ready. This can play out in all sorts of negative ways after the marriage. In many cases, the man ends up having an extramarital affair because he feels he did not get the opportunity to truly choose the mate he wanted. His hand was forced. He struggles with trusting his wife. What other things will she do without his permission that will affect his life?

Then there is the issue of children. Though a man may love his child, the hassle of dealing with an angry woman whom he cannot trust causes him to distance himself. He then deals with the pain of not having access to his child. He worries about the child's opinion of him as a father. He wonders if he will be replaced by another man. How much influence will he be able to exercise in the life of his child? Will his child struggle with its identity? Will the child blame himself because his parents are not together? On and on the inner conflict rages. Are you getting the picture?

Personal Confession

I will consider my heart condition carefully and not be ruled by it. I will make sound judgments and choices not based on my cravings, but on my purpose so I may fulfill my destiny according to God's design without unnecessary difficulties.

Men can avoid this lot in life by choosing to stay pure, and set the tone for spiritual leadership by becoming the high priest in the relationship and standing firm against the advances of a woman. Just as men test women, women also test men. Women's need for love and attention pushes them to dabble with your passion in order to find out if you are truly attracted to them or not. You would do well to let the woman know that, indeed, you are very attracted to her, but you want to honor God as well as her in the relationship. And you would appreciate her exercising self-control with you.

In the midst of the hunger for love, these very important things are not thought out. The heart justifies seeking after what it wants in the now without contemplating the consequences. The question you must ask yourself in these moments is, "Is my hunger real or imagined? How urgent is the cry of my flesh, and who is really in control? What will it cost me to indulge my flesh? Are these consequences I really want to bear?" Search your heart and be very honest. Remember, hunger passes.

The Self-Made Life

But let's get back to the main issue. Doing it yourself always results in the death of something: your dreams, the plans you had made for your life, joy, peace, fulfillment. Elimelech, the leader of the crew that went down to Moab, was the first to die. Could it be he did not do well in Moab either? I doubt that was the problem. After all, Naomi, his wife, did not die or even get sick. Perhaps he was sick at heart and wasted away in his soul until his body followed suit. When we move out of place, out of time, out of God's perfect design, we lose pieces of ourselves that we can never regain. We spend the rest of our lives trying to catch up with a plan we did not have.

What we must bear in mind is that when we decide to fulfill our needs in our own way, instead of waiting for the fulfillment that can only come from God, other people besides ourselves are affected. Naomi ended up a widow. Her sons were left without a father to be their leader and example. The patriarch, the head of the family, was gone and would not be replaced. God is the great Restorer, but why go through the unnecessary grief of incurring losses if we do not have to?

Choose the journey you want to take and stick to the path ordained by God. The quick fix only brings about more problems in the long run. Decide to trust God to make provision for you when it comes to love, and you will never go wrong. The old folks used to say, "He may not come when you want Him, but He's right on time." That is the gospel truth.

Remember, there is a season for everything. There is a time for planting, so sow carefully. There is also a time to let what you have planted grow. During this time, it may seem as if nothing is happening, but deep beneath the surface, beyond what your eye can see, something is indeed going on! The roots of what you have planted are digging down deep. In due season those seeds will sprout and bear marvelous fruit. Be careful how you select the woman in your life and be cautious of how the relationship progresses.

What would you like to harvest: joy, contentment, fulfillment? Then do not let your hunger manipulate the seed. You have been given the power of choice, a great gift from God. You can choose life or death, blessing or curses. Your decisions will dictate what you receive. If you are like Elimelech, confessing that God is your King, you will have to trust Him with timing as well as provision for your life.

Check your attitude toward God. Do you believe He loves you? Do you believe that He wants the best for you? Do you believe He knows what is best for you? Do you believe He is able to give you what you want as well as what you need in the same package? When you hire a painter, you do not help him paint the walls. No matter how long it takes him to finish his task, you leave him to do it because you believe he knows what he is doing. Sometimes waiting on God is like watching paint dry. It is hard to tell on the surface if anything is happening because there is nothing visibly changing before you, and yet, the results are lasting once the paint has set. If you are struggling with the concept of God's goodness and your own issues of self-control, these need to be your first areas of concentration.

The issue of lust will not be solved after you get married because it is deeper than just putting out an occasional fire. It deals with the state of the heart. Issues concerning your faith will not be solved after you get married because you will have different things to deal with that will require His help and intervention. Therefore, settle in your heart that God is good all the time and wants you to experience lasting love and fulfillment even more than you do. This is crucial to your spiritual and emotional health. If you never get this settled between yourself and the Lover of your soul, then truly you will die. And above all things, His desire for you is to live.

 The Facts on Women

➤ A woman will follow where you lead her. Plan your steps carefully.

➤ Women are looking not only for husbands; they are also looking for fathers for their children. Do not become a lover until you are a husband.

➤ Do not settle for an okay relationship just to pass the time away. When a woman gives herself to you—heart, mind, and body—she expects a commitment from you. She will feel betrayed if she finds out you led her on.

Consider This

- What things do you do to compensate for the love hunger you feel? What is the effect of your choices?

- What healthier choices can you make for yourself that will lead to peace and joy?

- Are you driven by what you want to *receive* or what you want to *give*?

- What choices can you make to redirect your desires so that you will bless other people as well as yourself?

◄►

The thief comes only to steal and kill and destroy;
I have come that they may have life,
and have it to the full (John 10:10).

3

Love at Any Cost

And she [Naomi] was left, and her two sons.
Now they took wives of the women of Moab: the name of
the one was Orpah and the name of the other Ruth....
Then Mahlon and Chilion [Naomi's sons] also died.

RUTH 1:3-5 NKJV

We are about to tackle what we settle for when we have limited our options by our own design. If Moab was the environment Naomi's sons were in, what other choice could they make regarding wives? Mahlon and Chilion ended up marrying women from Moab: Orpah (meaning "neck") and Ruth (meaning "friendship"). "Sickly" marries "friendship" and "wasting away" marries "neck," but marriage is still not enough to nurture these two men to health. They die. It becomes clear that marriage is not the answer in and of itself. Marriage is never the solution to our problems. As a matter of fact, it could make matters worse if our issues are not dealt with first. If we are sickly in our attitude toward life and love, and wasting away because we believe we are incomplete without a mate, nothing will change after the words "I do" are uttered. It is hard to imagine this, but an even greater loneliness awaits you after securing a mate and discovering she cannot help you feel any better about yourself. Many men shrivel up and die daily within the confines of what they just knew would be the safe haven of marriage.

These two men married women that the law told them they should not even *consider*. They were supposed to marry women from among their own people, women who had the same culture, background, and belief system. The struggle for two people to become one is usually less severe if they agree on most things starting out. Mahlon and Chilion's hunger led them to compromise their standards, believing they would find life. Instead they died slow, painful deaths, which is what happens to most relationships of this nature.

For believers in Christ, the issue of not being "unequally yoked" is not about race, but about spiritual culture and experiences. Both of you can be Christians and still be unequally yoked. Are you both on the same path, walking toward the light, choosing to obey God because you are committed to living according to His Word? That is the big question. Two cannot walk together unless they have agreed to do so (Amos 3:3). The bottom line is this: If you are not walking in the same direction in life, you will end up going separate ways. Whether you are a Christian or not, aligning yourself in a committed relationship with a woman who does not agree with your values and basic belief systems will be problematic throughout the life of your marriage. It will never be harmonious. Neither of you will be equipped to continue in a home where you disagree more than you agree.

I find more women than men in the difficult situation of being married to unbelievers. Or perhaps women are simply more vocal about it as they solicit the prayers of people at church to pray that their husband will come to a place of embracing a relationship with God. They are lonely and unfulfilled because they feel a gaping chasm between themselves and their husbands on the grounds of what they do not share. What seemed worthy of the risk before the wedding day gives them room to pause afterward. And let's not even speak about what happens after children enter the picture and become affected by one of their parents' lack of interest in spiritual things. It seems that men who venture beyond the church to find women end up in two categories. They either lead their spouses to Christ, or they compromise their standards in order to get the woman they want. The latter can be a rather hazardous choice.

Many single Christian men say women in the church are either too desperate or not as exciting and attractive as women of the world. This becomes the justification for missionary dating. This is what you are doing when you decide to recruit and save an unbelieving woman. Bad idea! Why are we instructed to avoid being unequally yoked? Because God knew the nature of the beasts that were joined together with this instrument.

Though you may convince yourself that you can influence your woman to come to Christ, the sad truth is, in most cases, this is not what occurs. Lack of success is usually due to the inability of the man to keep his standards high and not compromise his position or his flesh. This is what happens when you yoke a weak ox to a strong one. The strong one is not able to pull the weaker ox to match the faster pace. The strong ox compensates for the weakness of the other ox by stepping back and slowing its pace. After a while, its muscles that are no longer being used begin to grow weak, and it ends up in the same shape as the ox it was joined to.

The Valley of Compromise

It is just as easy to fall in love with a nonbeliever as it is to fall in love with a believer. The nonbeliever might score extra points in some areas, if we are really being truthful here. Let's be honest on how the relationship plays out if you are smitten with a woman who does not have your same spiritual commitment. You have a tendency to compromise, perhaps not sexually at first, but conversationally. You decide that you are not going to "push your beliefs" on her, so you remain quiet. You do not speak up when the conversation travels down a path it should not. You do not say things you should and you say things you should not. You almost end up apologizing at times for what you believe so she will not be uncomfortable. Interesting that you would sacrifice your own comfort level for a woman who has no respect for what you believe.

After your conversation gets watered down, your habits begin to decline. In an effort to prove you are flexible, you miss church or Bible class. You stop being transparent with your friends because you do not want to be held accountable. Once you become disconnected, it is easy to take the next step: physically relaxing. Entering into a sexual relationship before marriage brings condemnation. Once you have done it enough, your conscience becomes seared to the point you begin to justify your actions. Meanwhile, you fail to realize you have lost this woman's respect. Even the world is impressed when a man can stand up for what he believes without cracking. In her mind, you talked a good game in the beginning, but in the end she wore you down. She comes to the conclusion that Christian guys are like all the rest. It is simply a matter of time before they reveal who they really are.

The Bible clearly shows that whenever people compromised with those who did not share their knowledge and their love for God, the relationship ended in death. This could be death of joy, peace, and fulfillment, or perhaps even a physical sacrifice was made. The best example of this is Samson. When Samson married a Philistine woman, the affair ended in betrayal and a revengeful bloodbath. Later, when he got involved with a Philistine prostitute, he almost got caught in a death trap. People were lying in wait to kill him after he emerged from the prostitute's home. Even after that, he still had not learned his lesson. He ended up living with the infamous Delilah, another Philistine woman. This relationship not only led to his being blinded, but also to bondage and eventually death! Though God lovingly redeemed him before he died, perhaps he would have been around a little longer had he not made the fatal choices that he did. His love for foreign women cost him entirely too much.

A man has to understand that a woman can make or break him, propel him into the midst of his purpose, or rob him of his destiny. The man is responsible for steering the relationship, not allowing the woman to manipulate his flesh until he is reduced to a heap of compromise. He will give away things he can never get back.

How many times are we blinded by the emotions that flood us when we are with someone who makes us feel good, no matter how bad the situation may be for us? Self-deception quickly gives way to unnecessary pain when the relationship ends or fruit comes to bear that we did not want to harvest. It is time to take control of your life and guard your heart so that you do not grow sickly and waste away from bad choices and a lack of discipline.

Despite what your eyes see, God is not limited in His reserve of incredible women whom He has set aside for uncompromising men. Perhaps there is a test that must be passed first. How do you deal with your love hunger? Are you willing to become a disciplined eater? With whom are you hanging out? Where are you going? What is your conversation? All these factors could be limiting your options. I am not saying that you should not have any friends who do not

Personal Confession

I will not compromise my standards and settle for a woman who does not walk in agreement with my values just to have her in my life. I will hold out for the one who is right for me.

agree with your beliefs or lifestyle. After all, Jesus made dangerous friendships that the Pharisees, the religious watchdogs of the day, disapproved of. Yet He did not make these dangerous friends His close disciples. His inner circle was reserved for those who embraced the truth and willed to walk in it. He talked with those of the secular world, ate with them, and nurtured relationships with them for the sole purpose of turning their hearts to God. If your goal in your relationship with a woman who does not embrace what you believe is to draw her heart toward *you* and not toward *God,* you will lose on both counts.

The Value of Love

I find that women are taught a lot about self-esteem, but men, in general, are not given the same depth of teaching about knowing who they are or recognizing their value. When identity issues remain unsettled, coupled with a healthy dose of not trusting God to give him his heart's desire, it is enough to make him settle for anything! As I have often taught, God makes many references comparing us to precious jewels: the pearl of great price, gold refined, etc. If a man can grasp the concept of a woman being a rare and priceless diamond, then he should understand that such stones are not left out in the open. They are kept in the owner's secret place until a worthy man comes looking for them. Only people who know specifically what they are looking for are exposed to these incredible stones. They are not in a setting yet because each stone of great worth is set individually according to its worth and weight. The greater the weight, the stronger the setting must be to hold it.

For larger stones, the recommendation is usually made for them to be set in platinum—the hardest metal in which a stone can be set. It is a rare metal and used in 90 percent of its pure form. Only ten percent of other metals are added to it in order to make the setting hold. Gold is a softer metal. This means up to 40 percent of other metals are added to make it hard enough to hold a stone; therefore, the setting is not pure gold. The gold can soften from the heat of our hands and bend. Sometimes the prongs will lose their hold and the stone will be lost or have to be reset.

In essence, the setting (that would be you, Mr. Man) is just as important as the stone. If the setting is not up to supporting and protecting the stone, your union could be short-lived! A true jeweler knows the worth of his stones and will not discount them or place them in an unworthy setting. A real man will be willing to walk a life of discipline with his woman and do everything in the right order to gain her hand in marriage. He will not compromise her in any way, and vice versa. A woman who is not committed to Christ does not care about your soul or your convictions. She only cares about what she wants from you. And after she gets it, the rest of the story is not a pretty one. How many men, like Samson, have been swayed by a pretty face, shapely body, and sensual attitude and ignored God's advice? The nudging of the Holy Spirit tells you the woman you are involved with is not right, but you proceed to try to make her fit into your world anyway. It very rarely works. If it does not fit from the beginning, it never will. It is like buying a suit too small in hopes of losing weight.

Samson's parents tried to get him to rethink his marital choice, but he discarded their advice because he was intoxicated with the woman's beauty. He did not even know her that well! The media has done an incredible job of painting images of women that the average male will only see on TV. Men will go looking for those same images in real life. Unfortunately, minus all the makeup, special effects, and lighting, the average woman is a more realistic version of what really exists. The temptation to embrace the above-average, beautiful woman without taking the time to know the inner woman can be a big mistake. While there are many beautiful women who are just as beautiful inside as they are outside, there are also those who have not worked on their character because they did not have to. Take the time to find out which woman you are dealing with. Beauty fades and charm can be deceitful. It is best to see the entire woman as she is. You have more to protect than your heart. You have a destiny and purpose to protect. This is the root of your value as a man, and the very thing the devil would love to use a woman to destroy.

There is no perfect woman, but there is one who will be better suited for loving you and dealing with all the delicate areas of your heart and spirit. She will be handcrafted by God from the day of her birth to embrace you and fit just right. The imperfections that remain will be deliberately left by God. Why? Because it is the rough edges of two people that sharpen one another like nothing else can (Proverbs 27:17). If we allow ourselves to be used to temper the uncultivated parts of each other's spirit, we both emerge as better people, with a greater capacity for love and victorious living.

How do we find out what our value is? By looking into the Word of God and seeing what He thinks of us. I mean, if the King of kings says we have value, we better believe it! He says that we are fearfully and wonderfully made. What does that mean exactly? It means He had tremendous respect for His own creation, that even He had a sense of awe as He oversaw us being formed in our mother's womb. An even greater fact is the sacrifice He made to rescue us from our own sinful nature, literally from ourselves. The price He paid to ransom us from the grip of the enemy of our souls is inconceivable: the life of His own Son, Jesus. How many of us would be willing to allow our child to be killed to save someone else?

The Value of a Man's Strength

With so great a price tag on our lives, how can we allow those who do not realize or acknowledge our worth to claim our hearts? When Samson fell prey to Delilah, he loved her, but she did not love him. She was a woman of the world. Her values lay elsewhere. She was not interested in what she could give to Samson, but what she could get out of her association with him. In this case, it was money. She manipulated him, literally stole his strength from him, and left him to be destroyed by other people. She was not a woman to be trusted. His God was not her God. She did not place a value on spiritual things or the calling on his life. In the end, Israel was robbed of a judge who could have set them free from the grip of the Philistines—all because of a woman. Here was a man who failed to discern who he really was and understand his value to God, to others, and to himself.

Do not ever apologize for keeping a standard; instead, let it be your guidepost. Quietly evaluate your options and decide if the woman standing before you is conducive to how you see your life moving forward. If she is more of a distraction than an asset and is causing you to stray from your course, release her and move on. Just because she is not the one for you does not mean she will not be perfect for someone else. Be responsible enough to not leave unresolved wounds behind that make her a mess for the next man she encounters.

You might encounter several women who would be great mates for other men, even though they are not a good fit for you. Sometimes they will be wonderful for you, but you will not be good for them. Be honest with yourself and decide if you can give this woman what she needs in a relationship. Do not be selfish and keep her hanging on because all of your needs are being met. Love is a two-way offering. Both people should be blessed in the giving.

Bathsheba warned King Solomon in Proverbs 31:3 not to spend his strength on women or his vigor on those who ruin kings. Later in that chapter, she goes on to list the qualities that qualify a woman for serious consideration as a lifetime mate. We will look at this more in depth later. But for now, suffice it to say, that if the woman in your life causes you to question yourself, divides your thoughts, renders you inoperative, distracts you from your first intentions and plans for life, get rid of her. She is robbing you not only of your strength, but she is also sucking the life out of your purpose and distracting you from reaching your destiny. This is death to a man. Many athletes will tell you that before playing in a game they will abstain from relations with a woman. When asked why, they say it is because it saps them of their strength, and they want to be strong for the game. At that moment, winning the game is more important to them than a few moments of pleasure. You, too, must decide what is most important to you: winning the overall game of life, or grabbing temporary pleasures where you can from a woman who messes up your mind, messes up your life, and renders you ineffective to win in the marketplace, or anywhere else for that matter. Decide before you play the game what your priorities are and stay focused.

The young men I mentioned earlier in this chapter, Mahlon and Chilion, died in a place where they did not belong, caught up in relationships they should not have had. Though God is able to redeem anything, more often than not when two people are involved with conflicting wills, death is the outcome of the ill-fitted relationship. Something is not necessarily better than nothing if that something will eventually kill you. Take the time to list what you truly want from life and stick to your list. Do not allow hunger to talk you into taking an appetizer that will kill your discernment and appetite for the main course God wants you to enjoy. Remember, God's design for love is to increase our capacity to give life.

The Facts on Women

➤ A woman can make or break a man; therefore, not just any woman will do! Make sure she adds to your life and does not subtract from your quality of living.

➤ The enemy will use a woman to distract you from your purpose and rob you of your destiny. Check yourself and your productivity when involved with the woman in your life.

➤ If a woman begins leading you in the relationship, she will never stop. The way to earn her respect is to take the lead and keep it.

➤ Be clear on who you are and what your purpose is. Stick to your program unless God says differently. The woman for you will be a team player and know you are her assignment, and vice versa.

Consider This

- How do you find yourself compromising when your faith for a mate runs low?

- What is the common pattern you see running through all of your relationships with women? What is the root of your attraction to the same situation? What hunger have you not addressed?

- What is your sense of purpose or destiny for life? How can a woman contribute toward these things? What would the wrong woman do to get you off track?

◆▶

*He who is full loathes honey,
but to the hungry even what is bitter
tastes sweet* (Proverbs 27:7).

4
The Winds of Change

When she heard in Moab that the LORD had come to the aid of his people by providing food for them, Naomi and her daughters-in-law prepared to return home from there. With her two daughters-in-law she left the place where she had been living and set out on the road that would take them back to the land of Judah.

RUTH 1:6-7

*R*umor has it that patience wins the game of life. Naomi gets wind of the fact that the people she left behind in pursuit of a full tummy are still alive, eating, and none the worse for wear in spite of staying put. She, on the other hand, had suffered great losses in the land of her own undoing. The journeys we choose for ourselves, when we think life is not going as it should, often lead us down a detour even further away from our desires. Those who stay on course, no matter how much their longings cause their spiritual stomachs to growl, are able to smile at the end of the journey.

Oh, how I can relate! I recall an incident that was a marker for me in my own single life. After establishing a relationship with Christ and making the commitment to be obedient to His Word, the initial zeal of my newfound faith wore off and I found myself challenged in my personal life. Before I came to the Lord, I had always had a man in my life. As a matter of fact, I was living with someone before I became a Christian. His death was what propelled me into the arms of Christ. My new lifestyle definitely affected my dating habits. None of the men I went out with could wrap his head around the concept of celibacy. Small wonder because none of them was claiming to be a Christian! Needless to say, after a while my phone did not ring as often.

Not hanging out, dancing the night away, and meeting fun guys who never meant to be serious was not something I missed. However, I did miss having someone in my life to share my heart with. So I made a bargain with God. I told Him I could live a celibate life for exactly one year, and after that I would not be responsible for my actions! I am sure He got a big laugh out of my directive. I had some nerve back then. I am sure He celebrated my commitment to even that, which was a far leap from skipping over any page in my Bible that I thought was going to tell me that sex before marriage was a no-no. For some strange reason, I thought if I did not read about this, I would not have to be obedient to it. Fortunately, I could not get away from my own spirit where the law of God was already written on my heart, giving me an instinctual knowledge of right and wrong according to the One who had created me in the first place.

After making this proclamation, I made my second deal with my omniscient Father. He should save a famous musician that I had dated and give him to me as a husband. I would be willing to wait for him and consider no other man as long as God would hurry up. Well, He did not pay attention to any of my plea bargaining, and my misplaced expectations made the next several years bitterly painful ones. I was determined to stick it out with God, but I cannot say I did so joyfully. Actually, I became a character in the worst religious nightmare. I loudly judged people who compromised their lives and "lived in sin," not because I truly wanted them to walk in victory with God, but because I was jealous!

Yes, in hindsight I felt they were allowed to enjoy themselves and get away with it while I could not. I lived in fear of

God's wrath and the consequences of my sin, even though I was not sure what they would be. You see, in the back of my heart I harbored the hope that if I was a good little Christian "do-be," God would give me exactly what I wanted. I would score major brownie points with Him, and He would be so impressed by my goodness that He would have to cooperate with my agenda. But if I was "bad," I could kiss my dreams good-bye.

But alas, I had a hard lesson to learn. God did not owe me anything for my obedience. He does not bless us because of outward actions. He blesses as He is moved by our inner attitudes and His own determinations of what is good for us. He had already given the greatest blessing of all: the sacrifice of His Son, Jesus, for my silly sake. How dare I think He owed me anything else! The reality was *I* owed *Him* my obedience. That was the *least* I could do.

A hard lesson for a man to learn is that he is not his own source of genius, success, strength, anything. That is why it is crucial that you partner with God in this area of obedience big time. Talk it out, then *walk* it out. As you struggle with your sex drive or any area of lust in your life, know that it is God who will sustain you as you choose to live by His design. Here I am talking about years of being celibate, whereas the average male shudders at the thought of a month without sex. The world has led men to believe that sex is something they should be having all the time, and if you are not, you are not a man. God's definition of a true man is one who knows Him and masters his cravings to the point that he walks in total obedience—not by his own power, but by the grace of God and the empowerment of His Holy Spirit.

One of the biggest mistakes Samson ever made was overestimating his own power and believing he was doing God a favor when he won a battle. He forgot that it was God who had empowered him to win! Samson decided that his strength was of his own doing and not from God. So God said, "okay," and stepped back, leaving Samson to the fate of his hair. The end of the matter was not a pretty picture. After many tears and a deep, heartfelt repentance, Samson struggled to receive the forgiveness that God gave. But that was the easy part. For far longer than any of us care to admit, we hold ourselves hostage in the prison of our own unforgiveness after we mess up. Some people struggle to get back on the right track, while others resign themselves to the fact that they are just going to mess up from time to time until they settle down. God will just have to understand. But He does not. He is not going to lower the bar of His expectations toward you simply because you do not want to master the art of self-discipline. Instead, He will leave you to deal with the consequences of your actions, just as He did with Samson.

Yes, my friend, there is a day when grace runs out—not in terms of salvation, but in terms of our individual cycles of sin. There is a payday for those who continue giving in to the flesh and never truly repent. There are too many scary options in this arena that I know I do not even have to list. You know them already.

Starting from Scratch

So what is a man to do? How do you get back on track when you have taken an unhealthy detour and you cannot find your way out? Well, the first thing you need to do is own up to your actions. Be strong enough to say you had a hand in creating your own mess. If you are truly honest, you will have to admit that all the red flags were waving. You simply refused to heed them and hoped things would work out to your liking. Our Bible heroine Naomi did not claim ownership of her mess very well in the story I have been sharing. Even though she had the good sense to go back home, on two occasions along the way she blamed her lot in life on the Lord, without ever owning up to the fact that she was the one who had moved, not God. She was the one who had broken His rules and was now in a state of dismay and bitterness.

Repentance is not admission or even confession. It is turning way from your former actions. This means someone might have to be removed from your life. In order to repent, you must begin by confessing your actions in light of what God says about what you have done. This is where all rationalizing and justifying must be laid aside. When David finally confessed to his affair with Bathsheba, he said to God, "Against you

Personal Confession

I will not cast blame, but take responsibility for my decisions and mistakes, being honest with God and myself.

and you alone have I sinned!" even though he had also killed Uriah, Bathsheba's husband, in order to have her and cover the issue of her wrongful pregnancy. Most men struggle to balance their Christianity with their sex drive. There seems to be a casual attitude among some men who say, "It's a man thing. God doesn't really expect me to be celibate, does He? He couldn't really think it is wrong for me to follow my natural desires, could He?" The answer is yes to both questions.

There is no place in Scripture that frees men to follow their hormones while telling women to suffer until they get married. No, both men and women are called to live a life of purity as singles. Many men fall into the trap of thinking they are the only one trying to live a holy life, while all the other guys are having a good time. This one small trick of the enemy makes many men fold and give in to their passions. The result is always the same: a sense of growing distance between themselves and God, as well as increasing discontentment and diminishing discernment.

Perhaps you have strayed off the path of kingdom living in your heart. Sometimes our bodies are in the kingdom, but our minds are in the world. We go through the motions of holiness without emotion or passion, no longer motivated by our love for God. Out of duty, we toe the line, devoid of a grateful heart or a worshipful attitude. Not being a cheerful giver of yourself is just as bad as outwardly acting out what you are really feeling inside. After all, God knows your heart.

On the other hand, perhaps you have never made the commitment to love God or be obedient to His Word. But you are sick and tired of being sick and tired of experiencing countless unfulfilling relationships. You are left feeling empty and used, wondering if you will ever find true love. In or out of the kingdom of God, the answer is the same. Want different results? Do something different. Naomi made the crucial decision to leave the place where she had been. This is the first step to getting a new life and changing your circumstances.

A Turn for the Better

When I stumbled in the area of celibacy many years ago, I knew I needed a plan of action in order to restore my soul, so I decided to get out of my situation. I told the man I was seeing that I could no longer live a compromised life, and I was ending the relationship. I am not saying it did not hurt. What I *am* saying is that there were things more important to me: my relationship with God, my peace of mind, my spiritual and emotional state. Decide what is important to you. I chose to do what I had to do to get back to what I knew I could not live without: the blessing and favor of God on my life. In order to get there, a sacrifice had to be made. Sacrifices are not easy to make, but no pain, no gain. God understands that celibacy is a sacrifice that must be made willfully. This is why we are asked to present our bodies as living sacrifices that we might manifest the good, perfect, and acceptable will of the Father. In exchange for what He has done for us, it is a reasonable act of worship. I faced what my weaknesses were and set boundaries in order to avoid them. I urge you to do the same.

Examine your relationships. Do your friends and associates hold the same standard for living that you do? If not, rethink how much time you should spend with them. Though Jesus made quite a few questionable friends, they were not in His inner circle. The only ones in His inner circle were those who were seeking to walk in the light of God's Word. If you are trying to live one way, and your closest friends or the woman in your life live another, you will always struggle with your flesh. Your resolve will be weakened, and you will find yourself trying without success to navigate down a slippery path. No man can serve two masters—he will love one and hate the other (Matthew 6:24). The Spirit of God and the flesh will never be friends or abide peacefully together in the same house. One of them is going to have to yield to the other.

 **Personal Confession**

I will choose to live wholly by making choices that feed me life and blessing. I will determine to view things the way God sees them and govern myself accordingly.

The decision has to be made that you will make no provision for your flesh to rule over you. Remember God's commission to man in the garden? He was to have dominion not just over the creatures, but over himself as well. Need help? Choose to be accountable to a few spiritually mature friends who will speak the truth in love to you without being judgmental. If you spend time making sure you keep the log out of your own eye, there will be no time for pulling beams out of the eyes of other people. Purpose in your heart to stick close to the One who can give you overcoming strength.

Focus your attention on rebuilding your faith in God and the choices He makes for you. Study specific areas of Scripture that will help you to know how much He loves you. God is extremely particular about the wife He has in mind for you. He is very interested in that person being a perfect fit for you because of the plans He has for your life. Your choice of a mate could very well affect kingdom business. God will not settle for someone who will rob you of your strength and cause you to stray from the path of your destiny.

Trust God to give you not only what you need, but also what you want. He is able to combine the two into the perfect package for you that will make you exclaim as Adam did, "Wow! You are bone of my bones and flesh of my flesh!" (from Genesis 2:23). After all, if God knows how to give good gifts in every other area of your life, why can you not trust Him with this one thing? You do not have to accept a gift you do not want, but if God gives it, it will be good and perfect, I promise.

Next, cultivate a grateful heart. Be thankful for what you already have in your life: rich friendships, a supportive family, a wonderful network of people who believe as you believe. Nurture those relationships and live in the moment. Focus on the present moments of joy, and leave your future in God's care.

I believe that Ruth threw her future into the arms of God and decided to take the sure path by going with Naomi. This was someone she knew and loved, someone she could care for in the present. She also chose to embrace Naomi's customs, her people, and her God, which meant she was choosing to live God's way. She was taking a risk, and she knew it. What if the people in Judah did not accept her? What if she never found the love she longed to have again? She could not dwell on that. She just knew hanging out in Moab hoping she would get another husband was not the way to go. Nothing new is acquired in life without taking a risk. Those who do not take risks fall into boring routine and ultimately fade into oblivion.

Obviously, her sister-in-law, Orpah, was not into taking risks or trusting God enough to step out in faith. When Naomi told them they might fare better returning to their mothers' homes in Moab than going with her because she could not guarantee them husbands in Judah, Orpah opted for what she thought was a sure bet. She promptly made her decision to stay where she was. We never hear anything else about Orpah. I wonder if she ever got another husband, or if she eked out the rest of her days in her mother's house, regretting her decision.

Those who never stop to take a look at themselves and study their past patterns never see themselves as part of the reason why nothing new is occurring in their lives. This only leads to disillusionment, which paralyzes these people from pursuing purposeful living. The reality is this: You can move now or move later, but move you must. Nothing will happen until you get over yourself and make a move to get past your present mental attitude. Changing the way you approach relationships with women and the usual choices you make will be a challenge for you, but totally necessary to get to the next level.

Deciding to leave where you are is one thing, but getting back on the right path toward the heart of God and healthy living is another. It will take willpower to stick to your plan even when you do not see an immediate change in your circumstances or your joy level. You must determine to stay on the path daily, keeping the bigger picture in mind: peace, joy, and fulfillment that cannot be taken away by anything or anybody. Leaving behind unhealthy habits, relationships that are not going anywhere, unvictorious mind-sets, and even friends who feed you the wrong advice is a must to get on the road that will lead you to where you want to be in life.

One last thing: Do not romanticize the past. When Naomi returned to her hometown and her friends called her by name, she told them to call her Mara (meaning "bitter"), because the Lord had made life very bitter for her. She said she had left Bethlehem full but was returning home empty. But I thought they left because of a famine! How could they be hungry and full at the same time? Perhaps after she left and lived under worse circumstances, she came to realize life had been better before. Although they did not have everything they wanted in Israel, she had her health and her family intact, which was indeed a full life. Now she was empty. Many times after the fact, we look back on a bad relationship when we are alone and cling to the one good moment we had, forgetting all the negative things that were not conducive to our long-term happiness. We are tempted to return to a bad situation rather than wait for a better one. Do not go there. Stay on track! Men, you are just as bad in this area as women, perhaps more so because you are more fixed in your temperament—creatures of habit who do not like sudden changes.

Leave the idols behind—the false ideas on what your woman should embody, or even what position you should be in before you meet her. Real life can be a bit more basic in its makeup and not as demanding as your imagination. The fantasies that are made only for TV can distract you from the real person who is standing before you. Ask God to give you a heart that longs for who you really need in your life, and ask Him to help you recognize her when she comes along.

 The Facts on Women

➤ Women struggle with sexual temptation just as much as men do. They are simply conditioned differently by society to control their urges.

➤ A good woman is willing to help you be strong if you will solicit her help.

➤ The woman who will add blessing to your life will not deliberately lure you down the path of sexual sin.

➤ A woman will trust you and respect you more if you take the lead in maintaining purity in your relationship with her.

Consider This

- At present, where are you living emotionally, spiritually, and physically?

- What changes are you willing to make in order to ensure you live a life of purity until marriage? What boundaries will you need to set?

- What pressures, besides physical ones, cause you to give in to what your flesh wants? Are those pressures real or imagined? What can you do to dissipate them?

◀▶

For whoever wishes to save his life will lose it,
but whoever loses his life for My sake
will find it (Matthew 16:25 NASB).

5
Knowing Your Season

*So Naomi returned from Moab, accompanied by her
daughter-in-law Ruth, the young Moabite woman. They arrived
in Bethlehem at the beginning of the barley harvest.*

RUTH 1:22 NLT

I f you stay on track, you will get to a place of new beginnings,
hope, and fulfillment. But you have got to walk it out. Do not
try to go it alone; it is too difficult. Covenant to walk with
someone who has the ability to encourage you when you are
down, and vice versa. Most importantly, stop and take stock of
your life, and recognize the season you are in.

Discontentment usually comes from not understanding the
purpose or the season of our lives. I have found that my reading
audience spends more time worrying about why I am not married than I do. Marriage is not uppermost on my mind because I
understand the season I am in. Right now, I am sowing seeds. My
heartbeat, my greatest passion is to see men and women living
and loving victoriously. Why is it such a passion for me? Because
I was so miserable for so long that, when I discovered the secrets
to loving the life I was living, I just had to share them with other
people. I never anticipated how my commitment to sharing this
news would revolutionize my life or rearrange my priorities.

When the questions began about my marital status, some out of cattiness, some out of genuine concern, I had to stop for a moment to ponder why, because I had not really given it much thought. A husband is not and was not something I actively prayed for. I had, from time to time, actually met someone who was interesting and attempted to have a relationship. But when faced with the choice of finishing a chapter on a new book or going out to dinner, I chose to date my computer instead. I was frustrated when I had to divide my attention between a project and a man. Cute as he was, I just was not present. He felt it and I knew it. I realized it was not fair to see someone only when it was convenient for me. I would certainly be going against what I preached. As I consulted with God as to why I was at such odds, being ambivalent about having someone in my life, I was relieved to understand that I was in a different season of my life. For now, the call on my life was my first love. This season might change in the future, and I actually anticipate it will, but that is not where I am right now.

But enough about me. What about you? Think about where you are right now...in all honesty. Take a good, hard look at yourself. Consider your life and where it seems to be taking you. What seeds are you planting in order to get the life and the love you want? Perhaps this is your season for self-development. What is keeping you from pursuing your dreams in all earnest while you have the freedom to do so? While you do not have the obligations of a family to take care of is the time to live your life to the fullest, to experiment, to locate yourself, and to get on track with goals and pursuits. Men and women both say the same thing. They want a partner who is "about something." Yet, most people who say this are not really doing anything significant themselves. They are not willing to get the training and experience, be mentored, or work hard enough with their gifts and talents, so they settle for mediocre jobs that do not express who they really are. They remain unhappy, and then hope someone will come into their life and make them feel better.

This is a bit out of order. The key to attracting what you want is *being* what you want to attract. As a man who does not have his act together, you will never be comfortable with a woman who does. You will resent her accomplishments and feel belittled by them. Even if it does not matter to her, you will imagine that it does. So what are you waiting for? Get it together— she could show up any minute!

 **Personal Confession**

I will not rush through the seasons of my life, but will give my full attention to the tasks and opportunities at hand.

Now is the time to cultivate your interests and gifts. Take full advantage of your freedom. You will never have more financial freedom or more time than right now. Spend money, save it, and invest it wisely, cultivating a well-rounded and interesting life. Do not pursue different activities based on if there will be women there you can meet. Select what truly intrigues you. It is the best way to meet people who have similar interests.

Single Focus

More and more men are becoming single parents. I had a friend who was raising his two teenage daughters and a son. He was advised to focus on raising his children first and not consider marriage until they were in college and out of the house. He rebelled against this train of thought at first, but as several issues came up in his home, he decided this was the best route to take. Focusing on raising his children and dealing with a flourishing career took all his time and energy. The years flew by and, just as he was preparing his last two kids for college, he met the woman of his dreams. It was as if God timed it perfectly. His children were gone, and he was free to begin a new marriage with a clean slate.

If you are not a single parent, keep in mind that you are still in a season. While pondering what it is going to take for you to get what you want from God, consider the fact that God may want something from you! Perhaps He wants you to get into the flow of your destiny and fulfill your purpose before you meet your mate. If you do not, you might end up with the wrong partner. Though we all grow as we mature, we should be on the path toward our goals and dreams, having a clear vision of our passions and the things we want to accomplish in life.

Now is the time to become single-focused. Decide what you want your life to look like and prepare your dreams. This is the time to be planting seeds for your future, knowing that life will change drastically at harvesttime. A woman should know what she is getting herself into when she decides to marry you. To live one way, get married, and then completely rearrange your life is like false advertising and can be very jolting for your mate. If I had gotten married before I began my career as an author and speaker in full-time ministry, I doubt very seriously if the man I married would have been able to transition well. I still struggle myself with how much my life has changed. Gone are the long periods of languishing at home, entertaining friends, and spontaneously taking vacations. Instead, my life has evolved into a grueling schedule that even the hardy shudder to think of. It will indeed take a special man to deal with my life as it is, though I understand some adjustments will have to be made on my part in order to accommodate a meaningful relationship.

Marriage is so much more than an emotional bond. It becomes a business arrangement of sorts. When two people are called to be more than lovers, they must be partners as well. They must be able to support one another's vision and the call that is on their lives. A man must view the woman in his life as a part of his assignment to protect and nurture. I think of Joyce Meyer, and her husband, Dave. Dave prayed for a woman whom he could help. Today, he is her backbone. Though she is very famous and has a large ministry, she makes it clear to all that she could not do what she does without her Dave. Though not every man and woman are in full-time ministry, whatever their passion or vocation, they must be able to stand behind one another and champion one another's cause. It would help if you shared similar passions so you could be an active cheerleader on the sidelines, if not a willing assist. The only way you will know if this is true in your relationship is if both of you are actively living out the purpose for which you were created.

It was God who decided that Adam should have a mate. Until then, Adam walked and talked with God. It was his season for establishing his relationship with God and learning how to walk in authority on the earth. It was his season for learning the assignment he had been given for his life. As he applied himself to the tasks before him, without the thought of anything else, *God* decided that Adam needed help. God knows the exact time to introduce a mate who will complete you and take your life to another level, and He prepares her toward that end. In the right season, He will present her to you. Until then, apply yourself to your purpose and master your difficulties while you have time to work out the kinks without affecting anyone else.

I still chuckle at the fact that the area of my life that was the greatest cause of pain has become the most powerful part of my ministry. Truly, if we release our desires and become focused on making the most of the season we are in, God can transform our past failures and disappointment into present joy that will remain undisturbed, no matter how long it takes for the fruit we want to come into full bloom.

Now is the time to shout, "Carpe diem!" ("Seize the day!"). Work on yourself while the only person you really have to worry about is you. Do you like your body? If not, now is the time to change eating habits, get into an exercise routine, or do whatever it takes to become the you that you want to be. Remember, when you feel good about yourself, other people will, too. What about your finances? Are you in debt? Now is the time to get out of debt while there is just one of you. Take the time to clear your decks and save money so you are ready for a new life with new responsibilities and expenses.

Are you waiting to marry before you purchase a house? What if that never happens? Will you live like a nomad all your life? Speak to a financial counselor and get your affairs in order. Purchase something to rent out or to live in if you can, and begin to build a future for yourself. A woman will feel safer embracing a man who has his financial act together more than one who looks like he does not handle money well.

Is there something you have always wanted to try? Now is the time when you are not bound by sharing finances or time. Go for it. Experiment with life now while you have no one else to subject to your experimentations. If you have ever considered living in another city, you are free to go. Now is the time to be daring, to go where you have never gone, and do what you have never done. Open yourself to a world of possibilities and have the time of your life. Become an exciting person. Let your interests and experiences expand who you are.

You can be the one to mobilize all of your single friends. Start a travel club. Do a club savings program and pick a destination. Experience life to the fullest and get a world's-eye view of living. It will broaden your perspective and change you as a man. This season will pass, and having a partner might change some things so that it will not be possible to be so footloose and fancy-free. Why not take stock of what you could have and make the most of it this season?

The funny thing about seasons is that they may feel as if they will go on forever, especially if the one you are in is not your favorite season. But it is inevitable: This, too, shall pass. If you are faithful to embrace your season and plant the right seed, your moment of harvest is sure to come. When it does, it will yield your heart's desire.

The Facts on Women

➤ Women are attracted to men who have a sense of self and direction for their lives.

➤ Because women view men as knights in shining armor, women expect men to know some things that we do not. The savvy man who is well-rounded, with knowledge on various subjects, is exciting to a woman. Therefore, be well-read, if not experienced.

➤ When a man is unstable or unsettled concerning his career or what he wants to do with his life, it makes a woman nervous. If she is nervous, she cannot relax and entrust her heart to his hands.

➤ A man who is strong spiritually, sure of his purpose, and actively working toward the fulfillment of his destiny is the sexiest man on earth to a woman.

Consider This

- With what issues of life do you struggle? What areas of your life do you feel you need to master or set in place in order to be ready for a mate?

- Make a list of things you would like to try and places you would like to go. Map out a game plan for how you will accomplish these things.

- What season are you in? Into what purpose do you think God is trying to guide you before marriage?

◄►

There is a time for everything,
and a season for every activity
under heaven (Ecclesiastes 3:1).

6

Making Life Work

*Then she [Ruth] left, and went and gleaned in the field
after the reapers. And she happened to come to the part of the field
belonging to Boaz, who was of the family of Elimelech.*

RUTH 2:3 NKJV

*T*he plot thickens! While Ruth was not exactly looking where she was going, she definitely landed in the right place: in a field at harvesttime. Two people were in the same field with very different intent. Boaz was in the field making sure he would reap the most from the seeds he had planted. His agenda was to be diligent and responsible for what had been put in his power. What was on Ruth's mind when she headed for that field? Survival. Eating. That's all. She did not go looking for a husband. She did not even expect to find one. I am sure that Boaz was not looking for a wife either. The popular saying, "You will find what you are looking for once you stop looking," seems to be true in some respect. Sometimes when we cast our expectations to the wind without bitterness and discontent, I believe God is more moved to bless a heart that delivers His promises anyway.

In the world we live in today, many people have gotten things turned around. They look for the reward before having done any work. Everyone wants quick gratification. Not only

65

should a man be engrossed on the mission before him until God selects the time and the day for him to meet "her," but the woman also should be of the same mind-set. Ruth went to pick up the leftover grain being dropped by reapers in the fields. In other words, she was willing to work with what was available to her. We can either pin our hopes on the way we would like things to be, or we can work with what is in front of us. God has promised that if we are faithful with little, He will make us ruler over much (Luke 19:17). If you meet a woman who is more consumed with getting married than living life abundantly— flee! This woman will expect more than you will ever be able to give her. You will become her source for happiness, peace...you name it. The burden will be far too heavy, and you will fall beneath its weight.

How do we make our lives purposeful while we are alone? By applying ourselves to all we can do as singles. It is time to break the mold and cast down the misconceptions people have of singles. One popular assessment is that singles spend all of their time bemoaning the fact they are single and fail to be productive. I do not want to wear that mantle, do you? On and on it goes: Singles are engrossed with themselves...they do not take advantage of all their freedom affords...they are fiscally irresponsible, major consumers of anything that amuses from toys to clothing in order to appease their loneliness. Is this really true? If so, it is never too late to change.

Personal Confession

I will set my life in the right order and free myself to live my life to the fullest, whether I have a woman or not.

Sometimes what we have to work with in our lives does not look like much; however, it is a place to start. Ruth was into doing what was within her power: gleaning and getting what she could out of life. During this exercise, she had plenty of time to gather her thoughts and solidify the issues of her heart. Boaz was in harvest mode, also gathering and preparing for the future. In the midst of this atmosphere, the setting is ripe for two fruitful people to cross paths. Her life spoke for her. She had been through some things, but she was a survivor and a strong woman. Not only was she strong, but she was also soft, compassionate to people, totally unselfish, and giving. This was the reputation she had sowed for herself in this new field. Boaz's life spoke, too. It said he was a responsible and diligent man who had done his homework and was set for life. Naomi

Personal Confession

I will plant only what I want to reap in my life. I will understand that God has given me control over my affairs. When I partner with Him and walk in obedience to His Word, I will reap a fruitful harvest.

had spoken highly of him, and he was known at the gates as a man of integrity. I bet that all Ruth had heard about Boaz was confirmed when she met him.

What does your life say about you? Are you happy and whole, or are you miserable and laden down with all sorts of emotional baggage? Are your affairs in order, or are you always putting out personal fires? Your attitude will be revealed in the things you say, the air around you, and even in your outward appearance. Depressed people do not take good care of themselves, and it shows. Also consider what other people say about you.

You might not have it all together. You might have failed and made awful mistakes in the past. What you make of your life today can override all of your past issues and give you new grace that will open the door to walking in favor, acceptance, and love. God will cover your past and give you a new heart, a new life, and new and fruitful relationships. Harvesttime is about being fruitful—gathering the fruit from seeds sown the season before.

What are you reaping in your day-to-day life? How are your relationships faring? Now is the time to work on your interaction with people around you and make sure your connections are sound. If you have issues with your father or mother, please deal with them and resolve them before your mate comes along. Get counseling, confront whichever parent you have issues with, and do whatever you have to do to become healthy in this area.

Perhaps your father was not around, and you live with abandonment issues. Settle these things in your heart. Perhaps your mother was domineering or betrayed your trust in some way that causes you to be unwilling to completely trust a woman today. God is the only perfect Parent. Humans are guaranteed to fail. Do not hold them to a standard that is impossible to keep. Everyone deals from the deck with which he is familiar. Whatever your personal experiences, you are either paralyzed or empowered by them. Learn to look beyond the faults of people and see their needs. Work on your standing relationships and resolve outstanding issues. Keep short accounts and keep your heart healthy.

Attitude is everything when you approach life. People are watching. They are taking note. Are you happy? Can you hold steady even when life happens and you are hit in a crosswind? How do you deal with crisis and success? Do you harbor a superiority complex or a victim mentality? Are you so impressed with yourself that no one else has room to be? Is everything someone else's fault? Do you harbor an attitude of entitlement and get aggressive when things do not go your way? The reapers in Boaz's field saw him as a good and reasonable man, a fair and humble employer who knew how to deal with people in a respectful manner. He did not have to exert his authority. He merely wore it as a loose garment, and no one questioned it. He was sure enough in his success that he was free to notice the needs of other people. He was over himself. There is nothing more unattractive than a man who is full of himself.

Many times pride and fear of rejection stop a man from being desirable to a woman. The invisible shield is up, and people are bouncing off it! Unaware of the negative air you are pumping out, you reinforce your thinking that women cannot be trusted, and tighten your resolve not to let anyone in. You refuse to be vulnerable. Doesn't that word just make you tremble? Yes, even men are called to be vulnerable. We will talk about that later. The point is this: If we are not open, no one can come in—even those who want to. It is just too much work, and there are too many other easy options. So check your attitude. Ask some friends who will be honest with you what type of signals you send to people who do not know you well, and ask God to help you lower your defenses. You must learn to hide your heart in Him and allow Him to keep it safe while you continue being yourself, releasing the true you who lives within and wants to reach out to people. Remember, the woman that you fear will hurt you is also afraid of rejection.

If you have checked your attitude and find no real problems there, but it seems as if women are still not responding to you, and you are wondering what is wrong with you, never fear. I went through this for a season and I thought to myself, *Is there some weird growth on my forehead that I do not know about? Does my breath stink? What is wrong with me?* Finally, the quiet knowledge that God had put a hedge around me for a time to deal with just me became apparent. I began to rest in that season and allow Him to complete what He was doing. It was a time of self-examination and growth, of developing gifts I had overlooked, of literally blossoming as a woman! In the end, I was a much finer package to present to someone. In retrospect, I realize I was not ready and would have been a detriment to any man who would have approached me. A man also needs a season to walk alone and take stock of his personal kingdom. Figure out what you want and need in life, what you do not, and what you are willing to give in order to get what you want. Take some time and get with God. Then clear the decks and be open to love and new beginnings.

Living Life on Purpose

A lot of these issues will go away if your attention is focused where it should be: on moving forward. Concentrate on surviving in the present day and setting up a reserve for the future so you are ready for whatever comes or does not come. One of my favorite stories in the Bible is found in Jeremiah when the children of Israel were taken into captivity. As they sat around waiting to be rescued by God, a prophet by the name of Jeremiah was sent to tell them to get busy with the business of living where they were: building homes, farming the land, marrying, and so on. They were to live as if they were never going to leave, because the reality of the situation was that some of them would not be leaving. They were to remain in Babylon for 70 years! They were urged to be realistic about their circumstances and live life to the fullest anyway. Jeremiah concluded his message by saying that God knew the plans He had for them. God knows the plans He has for us, too, but He does not always give us the scoop right away. Does that mean we remain inactive until we get what we want, or do we move past survival mode to overcoming? The Israelites did not like where they were, but the question was, Could they trust God and settle down where He had them? The choice to merely exist versus living was up to them until God released them to return to Israel.

What is your motive for wanting a relationship? Is it because you want to have someone in your life to whom you can give your best, someone to love and cover and grow with? Is it more about what you have to give than what you will receive? With this attitude, you will avoid serious disappointment. If you are simply looking for a good decoration to wear on your arm to impress friends and coworkers, you can have that, but that will be all. In the end, it will not be enough to satisfy you. Do your homework. Know what you want and need in a relationship. Take the time to get to know the woman you are considering before you make any promises. Time tells the story about someone far better than the person herself ever could. Be consistent in your actions toward this woman and bide your time until you have seen all you need to know.

Ruth continued to glean in the fields of Boaz through barley season and wheat season. Let's say she was there about two months, perhaps a little longer, between July and September. Boaz did not try to move in for the kill right away. He watched and observed her. Although she was of interest to him, he put first things first. There were other important matters to pay immediate attention to. He set the atmosphere for her basic needs to be met, but he did not get involved with her during this time. No, he would be patient and stay on track. His focus was on completing the harvest.

Let's talk about this for a moment. What have you been sowing, and what are you harvesting at present? What do you have to offer to a woman? You see, Boaz was a man who was harvesting something. He was not in transition, deciding what he wanted to do with his life. He was a man with a plan, and he was working it. He had something to show for himself. Ruth did not have nearly what he had to show for herself, but what she did have was fortitude and resourcefulness. She was not looking for a handout. She was not waiting to be rescued. She was actively using what was at hand to make her life work.

The first rule in discerning if this woman is your Ruth is to see what her harvest looks like. If it is all drama—an accumulation of unfruitful relationships and dreams that she is still unsure of because she always hoped she would have a husband, then this is not the woman for you. I know men like to rescue women. Please make sure you do not attach yourself to a woman that you will need to be rescued from later. I also know that men love to feel needed, but there is a difference between being her hero and being her oxygen. The woman God brings into your life will have something to add to your life. She should be in harvest season in her own life and have good spiritual fruit to show for it: kindness, goodness, patience, gentleness, faith, love, joy, peace, humility, and self-control, as well as physical fruit. She should come into your life as a confident woman, a good gift, because she knows she has something to offer. She should have her own resources and gifts to bring to the relationship. You will attract what you are. Decide carefully what statement you want to make, and sow accordingly.

 ## The Facts on Women

➤ A woman looks to a man for stability. Inconsistency is frightening to her and causes her to question your intentions toward her.

➤ Consider that if a woman has cycles of drama and upheavals in her life, these will probably continue. If she is always a victim, at some point she forsook wisdom and became a volunteer. You will now become a part of the next dramatic episode.

➤ A woman who is fruitful in her endeavors and successful in her business is an asset to a man. Be secure enough to celebrate her accomplishments because you will also reap from them as her partner.

➤ Check the temperament of the woman to whom you are attracted. Is it all about her, or does she care about other people? This is a major sign of how your life together will play out.

Consider This

- How are you preparing yourself for marriage? How will you be a blessing to a woman?

- What things could you be working on right now to improve your quality of life?

- In what ways are you already a good candidate for marriage? In what areas can you improve?

◆▶

Finish your outdoor work
and get your fields ready; after that,
build your house (Proverbs 24:27).

7
Recognizing the Woman of Your Dreams

*Then Boaz said to Ruth, "You will listen, my daughter,
will you not? Do not go to glean in another field, nor go from here,
but stay close by my young women. Let your eyes be on the field
which they reap, and go after them. Have I not commanded the
young men not to touch you? And when you are thirsty, go to the
vessels and drink from what the young men have drawn."*

RUTH 2:8-9 NKJV

*E*very woman dreams of her knight in shining armor coming
to carry her away on a white horse. As little girls, women are
groomed to expect it. Perhaps men have similar dreams of
finding that beauty who takes their breath away and fulfills all
their needs. I always wondered what men really thought after
viewing a movie called *The Stepford Wives* years ago. It was a
frightening thought that men merely wanted women who were
beautiful, soft-spoken, domesticated, cooperative, and with no
minds of their own. This seems to project that men, in a way, are
afraid of women, afraid of the power we have over them. Since
then, many men have admitted this to me. It breeds distrust on
a very deep level and makes many a man conflicted when he
finally meets the woman for whom he is looking. Can he really
give his heart to this woman and trust her to hold it? I realize

that contrary to popular belief, a man's love runs very deep. He has to be careful where he steers it.

The reality is most women are asking themselves the same question. In the end, everyone—men and women—wants the same thing. So why is it so hard to find? Could it be a case of misplaced expectations? Men have a tendency to file women in a rather odd fashion. There is the friendship file, the plaything file, and the forever file. It seems that the women in the friendship file completely miss out on a chance to be in the forever file. Why? Because, "Well, she's too good of a friend. I wouldn't want to mess up our relationship," or "She's not my type." This train of thought has caused countless good catches to be sorely overlooked.

Consider what you truly want when it comes to love, my brother. If you want a friend and companion who will have the heart and the love you are looking for, then it is time to kill the fantasy and consider a good woman that you genuinely enjoy being with. You will need to be with your best friend on the days when you are not in love. A marriage can go a long way if you are with someone you actually want as a companion.

I can use my own brother as an example here. For years, he was close friends with the woman who became his wife. We could not get him to budge toward her romantically. She was not "his type." Physically, she was the exact opposite of the women he had pursued in the past, but they had such a good time together. He felt safe with her. He could tell her anything. Well, finally our family took a trip together, minus his friend. The entire trip was peppered with my brother's observances of what a great time Gina would have had if she were present. Finally I told him, "Listen, I think you like Gina more than you realize. If I were you, I would go home and grab her before she comes to her senses about waiting around for you and kicks you to the curb!" He went home and did exactly that. You could not meet a happier man today. He thanks God every day for giving him a wife who is his best friend to boot.

Who is Ruth? What does she look like? Well, do not let this scare you, but she usually does not look the way you expected her to look. No matter what she looks like on the outside, her heart will look better than you ever dreamed it would. Will God make you fall in love with an ugly person? No, He will not. He cannot and will not make anyone fall in love with someone. This would be usurping your free will. However, He can help you change your priorities. In the end, someone might look a lot different to you through the eyes of love. And good things do come in the most interesting packages....

Let's discuss a few nonnegotiables. What appeals to you about a woman's outward appearance is subject to change, but there are some inward characteristics that should always be present. These inner traits separate the women from the girls. Men and women generally have a problem. It is called a broken chooser. You get all excited over a woman's hourglass figure and beauty without noticing that she is just a pretty house with no one home. She has no conversation, just a whole lot of zing. She is so fine, but her attitude is downright ugly. She knows how to work a man, but she is very self-involved; therefore, her talk is always all about her. You should be able to deal with your stuff on your own. She is sweet and nice, but she has unresolved issues from a past relationship. Or, there is non-stop drama in her life that begins to get you worried. Last, but not least, she needs you to rescue her on almost a daily basis. What did she do before you showed up? Am I crunching on any toes yet? If a woman has one or more of the above traits, the woman you are looking at is not for you.

What type of woman is? First of all, she is in your corner. She is interested in you and in what is going on in your life. Even if she does not understand everything you do, she makes the effort to know who you are and what is important in your world. She is a team player—she wants to partner with you and support you in your endeavors. She actually hears you when you speak because she is really listening. She will be your friend and confidante, your co-conspirator. She will be the one who makes you want to be better than you already are, not because she asks, but because you are compelled to step up to the plate. You will know her when you see her because she will be different from any other woman you have ever dealt with, yet she will seem strangely familiar, as if you have known her for a whole lifetime already.

The Heart of a Woman

Check for the Ruth signs. Let's call them the five C's: clear, caring, committed, consistent, and complete. Throw out chemistry. That phase will rise and fall. What you want are things that are foundationally important to you. When you receive what you want from a woman, your desire for her will follow.

How does she view herself? Your woman should be clear on who she is and what is important to her. She is confident and has made peace with herself and with God. She does not rely on outward stimuli—men or things—to be her source of joy and peace. She has the joy of the Lord that does not fluctuate based on outward circumstances. When it comes to you, she knows what she has to offer and does it freely, without the expectation of a return. What she gives flows naturally from who she is. Her spirit, her conversation and encouragement, her friendship and caring are all genuine, a mere extension of her inner character. If you marry this woman, she will regard you as her assignment in life and will seek to help and not hinder you all of your days.

How do other people view her? Those who should never have considered her held Ruth in high regard. Does the woman in your life have long-standing, committed relationships with her friends and associates? What do her coworkers or employees say about her? Do they speak highly of her and commend her character and integrity, or do they make jokes about her habits and shortcomings? This is a big giveaway. Is her family life filled with drama and misunderstanding, or does she walk in harmony with her siblings and parents, especially her father?

A woman who loves her father and her brothers is an excellent prospect for a wife. If her father was not around, make sure she has settled her issues concerning him. A woman will either love men, be antagonistic toward them, or be uncomfortable with them, based on how her relationships with the men in her family have gone. Some of these things will take time to find out, but keep them in mind.

After inquiring about Ruth, Boaz then approached her. She did not approach him. Men find aggressive women attractive and interesting. However, most men do not want such a woman in a long-term relationship when they discover that the same woman who started the relationship is still running it. Men, I know you suffer with fear of rejection, but understand and know that the woman you are looking for, because she is a lady, is not going to approach you. She is clear about her place as a woman and likes a man who knows how to be a man. She is waiting to be found, and it is your God-given job to do just that. The Bible clearly states that *the man* who finds a wife finds a good thing. The man does the finding.

It is time to get bold and go after what you want. One of the saddest comments women in the church have about men is that they are all wimpy and weird. It is as if they all came to Christ, and in an effort to live holy lives, they lost major parts of their masculinity. They used to know how to talk to a woman. Now they have wooden conversations and are afraid to venture past a conversation about Jesus. What is up with that? God has called you to be yourself, while allowing Him to live in you. Yes, a woman's figure should still make you turn your head. Yes, you should still appreciate beauty. Yes, you should still pursue a woman if you like what you see. It is time for you to get back to your calling and once again reclaim the art of pursuit. Nothing worth having comes without taking a risk.

Now that you have approached this woman, what should you be looking for? What is her initial response to you? Is she happy to see you or is she hiding behind her friends? Women are pretty obvious, for the most part. Their eyes give them away. If she is shy, you might mistake her low-key response to be one that signals a lack of interest. Do not cave in immediately. Find a question to ask her that requires more than one word for a response, and draw her out. Women are just as confused about the mating ritual as men these days. They do not know if they should keep their cool or let it all hang out. But if you are really interested in this woman, then you must focus on her. If you are Mr. Personality, you might be tempted to ham it up for her friends to try to get on her good side. Don't. She will be much more flattered if you are pleasant with them, but more obviously interested in her. This sets her apart as special to you among her friends.

You might choose to not even dwell that long in the midst of her group, but let your intentions be known. You think she is beautiful, she caught your eye, and you would like to get to know her better. Could you give her a call sometime? Would it be possible to do lunch or dinner, whichever is most comfortable for her? Some women will give you their number; others will ask for yours. Why? She might be uncomfortable with giving out her number. She does not know if she likes you yet and does not want someone that she might not be able to get rid of in possession of her number. On the other hand, this might be a test to see if you are married. If she can have access to your

Personal Confession

I will reclaim my place as a man. I will not fear the pursuit, but will regard it as an adventure where the ultimate prize will be claiming my bride.

home phone, this reassures her that the decks are clear. Maybe then she will relinquish her phone number after her first call to you. Now that the game has begun, make plans for dinner after work. It is time to begin taking notes.

I would not call this a date yet, because nothing has been carved in stone. There have been no promises—nothing is guaranteed. This is what they call in the modeling world a "go-see." You are going out to see if you like one another. That is all. You have way too much data to collect before you even decide you like her. What you see is not necessarily what you get, so leave your heart at home. Now is not the time to give it away. First, find out if she is a caring person. This is important. What is her attitude toward other people in general? Is she a compassionate and sensitive person? If this is part of her character, that is a good thing for you. Now let's get more personal.

The Mating Dance

What does her body language and conversation reveal to you? Is she interested in who you are? Does she want to know all about you? I have to confess here that I blew it in this department with a man I really liked. I was more prone to listening to people talk about themselves and allowing things to be revealed about them without my help. I figured that was actually the best way to find out who they really were because they would talk about what was most important to them first. He, however, decided I was not that interested in him because I did not ask enough questions. Nothing could have been further from the truth. He was all I thought about. And even though I left the pursuit totally up to him, I was still totally responsive to him. I was not just happy when he called; I was thrilled to hear his voice.

Why am I telling you this? Because sometimes a woman does not feel free to ask questions. She might have been raised to see that as prying. Give her permission to ask you questions by asking her what she would like to know about you. I also find that question-asking seems to be a cultural thing. White people ask a lot of questions when they meet you. I have to admit that it makes me a bit uncomfortable when I meet someone for the first time and the barrage of questions begins. In the black culture, the unspoken rule is that it is rude or nosy to ask too many questions. So even if we are curious, we simply will not ask. We will wait until you either offer up the answer in the course of natural conversation, or until we feel close enough to you to ask the question without it seeming offensive.

If a woman is not asking you questions, what are the other signs that she is interested? Are you holding her captive, or are her eyes straying around the room in search of something interesting? Is she responsive to your questions or giving clipped answers? Is she relaxed in your presence, or trying to put as much space between the two of you as possible? Is she caring in her posture toward you? Does she touch your hand or shoulder just to have contact with you? Is she noticing little things about you? Is she excited about what you are excited about in your world? Does she thank you for the evening? As long as the evening is not all about her, it is safe to say that she probably likes you. What that means for you is that follow-up is important.

When a woman likes you, she really wants to hear from you the next day. Calling a week later throws her off-kilter and leaves too much to her imagination. The more room she has to rehearse different scenarios of why you have not called sooner, the more wary she will be of you and make your work harder. Simply ask if it would be all right for you to call her tomorrow. If you know you cannot, tell her that you will be busy for a few days but would love to call her again, if that would be all right. This will set her at ease because she will have your word to rest on. Which brings up another point. Be a man of your word. Do not make promises you cannot or will not keep. To the opposite extreme, don't start habits you cannot maintain. Don't barrage her with calls and then slack off once you get comfortable. That will make you highly suspect in her eyes.

By the way, now is not the time to get all deep and spiritual. Did you just gasp? I am just keeping it real! You should *be* spiritual, not have to prove you *are* spiritual by what you say. Jesus had general conversations with people. He opened the door for deeper conversation, but He allowed those He spoke with to choose when they were ready to go there with Him. Ask general questions, if you must, but forego a pop quiz on Scripture or a dissertation on the Holy Spirit. You will seem impressively spiritual, but religious and boring. For now, this woman just wants to accumulate basic information about you. Are you nice? Do you have a sense of humor? What do you do? What are your interests? What does your picture of the perfect life look like? Do you like her? That's it. There will be plenty of time for all the important stuff later. Who she is spiritually will be revealed through her conversation and how she handles herself on your evening out.

Personal Confession

I will not allow my imagination and desires to overrule the reality of who this woman really is. I will use my head, as well as my heart, and guard my affections until I know they can be released.

Now you need to check out her commitment level. What does her life look like? Is she passionate about her friends, her work, her relationship with God? If she is, she will be passionate about you, too. If her life has been a revolving door of relationships, jobs, and locations, she has not mastered the art of commitment. Commitment is not something that can be departmentalized. It flows through every area of your life. I realize that a lot of men tend to be intimidated by what they view as "powerful" women—those women who have garnered success in their field and made their own mark in their career sphere. You need to realize that "powerful" women need love, too. As a matter of fact, I would even venture to say that many of them are powerful because they have to be. No one has been there to give them the things in life they wanted, so they worked hard to get them for themselves. This does not mean they do not need a man. In most instances, they need one even more. As you begin to reach out and fill in the blanks in her life, to anticipate her needs and fulfill them before she has a chance to do it for herself, you will see this woman start to relax and allow you to take over. She is a relieved sister! She might not hand over the reins willingly at first because she is not sure that you will stay, so understand her reluctance to let you do the driving. Reassure her that it is all right for her to let go because you will be around for the long haul.

The Ways of a Woman

You have been enjoying her company for a while, but at some point you must move past enjoyment to commitment. A woman needs consistency and certainty in her life, especially if she is modeling consistency to you, as in keeping her word to you and being the sort of woman who does not disappoint you and is considerate of your needs. She is there for you and is reliable. She is not moody or constantly changing her mind. There is a big difference between spontaneity and being flighty and irresponsible. She makes you feel as if you can truly count on her. If these are things she is bringing to the table, she expects them to be returned.

The man is responsible for the relationship. Boaz told Ruth not to go gleaning in anyone else's field. It is up to you to let this woman know what your intentions are. If they are about courtship, you need to let her know and not leave her to assume. As a spiritual man of integrity, you must be intentional in your dealings with a woman and consistent in your follow-through. A woman has the ability to assimilate into a relationship even before a man has made it clear to her that they are indeed having a relationship. Be responsible for her heart and let her know if she should hang onto it or allow it to rest in your hands. The simple rule for relationships is you should give what you want to get. God is very fussy about how men treat His women.

Last, but not least, is she a complete woman? Was she complete before you found her? She should be. If she is, she will never burden you with false expectations. She will be an asset to you because of her strength and her peace. This woman has groomed herself to be a partner to a man. She not only takes good care of herself, she also knows how to make a house a home. She knows how to cook, even if her repertoire is limited. She is all about caring for you and nurturing your spirit and your mind before and after the wedding. She is a Proverbs 31 woman, understanding the seasons and purpose of her life. She understands what a "helpmeet" is, and is a willing candidate. This is the woman who releases a man to trust her with all of his heart, to finally know he has found his way home.

 The Facts on Women

➤ The man who takes charge earns a woman's respect. Once you have her respect, you can earn her love. If you lose her respect, you lose her love.

➤ Secretly, every woman wants a man who will take the lead in the relationship and make her feel safe.

➤ A woman is just as fearful of rejection as a man is. When a man does not keep his word, even in the small things, it ruptures her trust.

➤ If a woman cannot trust you, she will not release her heart to love you.

➤ Women were created for relationship. Their hearts settle this area quickly when they feel they have met the right man. Be clear in your intentions so there is no confusion on the status of your relationship.

Consider This

- What type of women have you allowed yourself to settle for in the past? Are they truly what you wanted or deserved?

- Do you walk the walk? Are your actions consistent with what comes out of your mouth?

- What would you say your false expectations have been in reference to your relationships? How would you now prioritize your needs differently?

Who can find a virtuous woman?
for her price is far above rubies
(Proverbs 31:10 KJV).

8
Turning the Tide

*Then Naomi her mother-in-law said to her, "My daughter,
shall I not seek security for you, that it may be well with you?
Now Boaz...is winnowing barley tonight at the threshing floor.
Therefore wash yourself and anoint yourself, put on your best
garment and go down to the threshing floor; but do not make
yourself known to the man until he has finished eating and drinking.
Then it shall be, when he lies down, that you shall notice the
place where he lies; and you shall go in, uncover his feet,
and lie down; and he will tell you what you should do."*

RUTH 3:1-4 NKJV

*T*his chapter is loaded with goodies, so we will go through it
carefully. When it is time to close the deal, a lot weighs in the
balance. It pays to make the right moves. The first thing to
master in a relationship is being sensitive to the right time.
Every season has signs to let you know when it is coming to a
close. In spring, it stays light longer; in the fall, the leaves turn
on the trees and eventually fall off; in winter, it gets dark earlier.
In the cycle of love, the more she cares for you, the more urgent
her need to know your intentions will become. She wants to
know if the investment she is making is worth it, or if she
should cut her losses and retrieve her heart while she can. Now
is not the time for you to flee. Be sensitive to her need for reas-
surance from you.

When love is in bloom, do not just languish in the feeling. You must be mindful of the signs so you will be ready for what comes next. This, of course, will not be totally left up to you. You must stay sensitive spiritually and keep close to the heart of God. He will always let you know what time it is. In Ruth's situation, it was Naomi who decided what should happen next. You might say, in a way, Naomi could be an illustration of how the Holy Spirit works in our lives. When God decides it is time for something to happen, He will, through His Spirit and sometimes through the nudging of other wise individuals, instruct you in the way that you should go.

The best approach is to seek God and find out what He has in mind for you before proclaiming what you are going to do. "In his heart a man plans his course, but the LORD determines his steps" (Proverbs 16:9). When God decides it is time for something to take place in your life, watch out—nothing can stop it from coming to pass! What would signal that it is time to move to the next level with your relationship and commit to marriage? Not just when you decide you can no longer contain yourself because you think it is better to marry than to burn. No…there is a lot more on the line than that—mainly your life, your purpose, your destiny.

When God chooses the time, He will also do the mate selection (that is, if we allow Him to). Naomi, per the Spirit of God, selected the time and the mate. She decided it was time for Ruth to have stability and security in her life. They could not live off her gleaning forever. For the woman, God decides when it is time to establish another level of security in her life and furnish her with a covering. With the man, it is a different purpose altogether. It has to do with his mental, spiritual, and physical well-being. When God decides you need assistance in order to live through the next season of your life more effectively, He will set things in motion.

God decided Adam needed help, and Naomi decided Ruth needed help. I often tell singles, "You do not need help doing nothing. Get busy doing what you were created to do, and that will propel you into position to meet your life partner." God creates teams. He created the animals two by two. Jesus sent the disciples out two by two. King Solomon said that two were better than one because they would have a good return for their labor. Teamwork gets things done. No man or woman is an island. One cannot bear fruit alone. It takes two, planting seeds together, to get a mutual harvest.

Completing the Harvest

In order to move to the next level of life, you must complete your assignment for the season you are in. How will you know when it is complete? You will not know until God says so. If you are applying yourself to life in the right manner, you actually will not care because you will be so engrossed in your present mission or project. You will then sense change in the air and know something new is happening, although you do not know exactly what. You will feel a sense of conclusion and mission accomplished. The season will change in your heart first. You might even feel some discomfort. Growing pains, I call them. You may not know what you are ready for, but you know you are ready for something else. This is how God will begin to condition your heart to receive the next phase of your life. When Adam awoke to find Eve standing there, he knew who she was and why she was there. He named her and embraced her. This is why it is so important that the season in the man's and woman's life has had the time to be completed and bear fruit. There will be no guessing games. Something deep in your spirit will click. You will know and recognize your Eve or Ruth and be ready to claim her.

Naomi decided Boaz was the perfect match for Ruth because he was family. He was from her own people. Oneness and being a part of each other has a lot to do with the similarities of the partners. Small wonder God created the animals after "like kind." Though opposites often attract, it is the similarities that keep couples together. Things they agree on build bridges that they can cross to their dreams. A house divided will fall. The more you have in common, the better.

Naomi expertly noted it was the end of the harvest season. It was time. Ruth could not go any further in her gleaning. The fields were stripped bare. Boaz had harvested all that he could and had a great return for his labor. There was nowhere to go except to the next level of living. When a man reaches that place where he has tasted accomplishment of a portion or the whole of his dreams and stands basking in the afterglow asking himself, "Is this all there is?" it is definitely time to add a new dimension to his life. This is where you get might get tempted to coast and skirt around the issue of pursuing a committed relationship. *Perhaps I should just enjoy my new accomplishments and freedom. How will I know if a woman really likes me or what I have?* Do not be deceived. The enemy of your soul can cause you to miss the next bend in the road that you should take. It is time to move beyond yourself and embrace another person. Otherwise, you will become stuck.

Personal Confession

I will be cognizant of the seasons of my life and sensitive to the times. I will not lag behind or try to run ahead. I will practice thriving and fulfilling my call in the season I am in.

There comes a time in a man's life when he becomes aware of the fact he needs a wife in order to get to the next level in life. That is when mating season begins. A word of caution here. When the alarm sounds in a man's mind, he is off to the races. He wants to get this mission accomplished as quickly as possible, and move on to the next item on his list to be settled. I know you men are task-oriented, but you cannot treat this area of your life like a task. Why? Because selecting the wrong person for this very important spot in your life can render you out of commission for all the other things left on your list to complete. Remember that Delilah cut Samson's career short!

The Perfect Soul Mate

Men and women share a common fantasy about what we call a "soul mate." Let me clear this up for you. There is usually in the life of every man an encounter with someone who seems to fit so perfectly that it is almost like being with himself. But it seems this is the person who does not remain. For the rest of your days, you think back on her with fond remembrances and wonder if you will ever meet another woman like her, another soul mate. I heard a preacher say once that you do not need someone just like you because if both of you were alike, one of you would be unnecessary! Good point, but consider another. If you are both alike, then you have the same weaknesses. There will be no one in the mix to balance you out. This could be a problem if you are not good with finances, or details, or a host of other things that make life run smoothly. So you had an encounter with someone who actually did nothing to promote growth in your life, but you were simply happy, happy, happy! You had good chemistry, good times, good everything. That is not how real life goes, is it?

Internalize this for a moment. God is your Soul Mate. From the moment He breathed the breath of life into your being and you became a living soul, your spirit naturally longed to be held in an eternal kiss with its Creator. This longing for a connection to satisfy us is rooted in our desire to be joined to God. Once you realize this, you can know you have already found your Soul Mate. You need to have patience to wait for a companion handpicked by God to not only help you, but also to stretch you and bring out the best in you.

Taking Care of Self

In the meantime, there is plenty of work for you to do while you wait, like getting yourself together. If your woman has to be a good thing, so do you. What do you want? Gorgeous? Easy on the eyes? The body beautiful? We read about Esther preparing to meet the king for 12 months before their first date. The emphasis always seems to be on the woman preparing for the man. But what about men getting themselves together for women? Your appearance, grooming, and style are important to us, too!

Let's focus on you. How do you feel about your appearance? We have dealt with your inner qualities a lot, but now it is time to deal with the outside—the first glimpse of you that anyone sees. In order to get a woman to respond favorably to you, she has to like what she sees. Let's get real. When a woman walks into the room, it is not her spirit that turns your head in her direction. It is her outward appearance. You do not turn to your friends and say, "Ooh, what a nice heart she has!" No! You say, "My, my, now that's a fine woman there!"

You take note of her height, weight, grooming, clothing, and the way she carries herself. Does she have a nice smile, great eyes, nice hands, good body? Am I telling the truth? You take stock of that woman from head to toe, and then decide you want to get more information. On the flip side of this equation, a good woman, who might not be as fine, can still win your heart with her ways. Women do tend to be moved more by what they hear, but let me tell you, looks help. Unfortunately, the older you are, the more a woman expects you to have developed fashion sense and good grooming habits. She does not feel this is something she can overhaul if you are over 30. In her mind, you are pretty set on your journey by then and would not welcome her rearranging you. And to tell the truth, she is right.

Taking care of yourself is the best investment you can make in yourself. You can be the most wonderful person in the world, but a woman will never find that out if there is not something about you that grabs her attention. Take the time to nurture your body as a man. Not everyone is going to have six-pack abs, but some sort of exercise is crucial to your well-being, even walking. It helps your posture, your heart, your energy level, and your skin. Your overall body profits from exercise. You will feel better about you when your body feels good. Many men and women are suffering from fatigue because they have not released enough energy to create energy in their bodies. Do not focus on being a supermodel; just focus on being fit and healthy. Women can be fairly forgiving of men who are not built like a bodybuilder. But in today's world, everyone is a little more body conscious than in years gone by.

Examine your eating habits. Has food become your sanctuary during your singleness? This is one sanctuary that can turn into a lonely prison if you continue to seek solace there. Do not beat yourself up about where you are physically. Just begin to get your body back on track. Find out what works for your body type, get on a healthy eating program, and determine to take control over your appetite and body.

Dressing for the Part

Because women are so conscious of dressing nicely for men, most women think that men should do the same for them. Every woman wants a man who "wears well" in public. Many a good man has been passed over because of the wrong sweater or the wrong shoes. My suggestion here is to ask a brother whom the ladies consider to have great style where he shops and get the salespeople there to help you with your selections. Or ask a sister with good taste if she would like to help you out with selecting a few pieces for your wardrobe. Women love being invited to do this task! First of all, they love to spend other people's money, even if it is not for them. Secondly, they love making men over. Ask her to give you an honest assessment of your style and submit yourself to the makeover, knowing you do not have to lose who you are in the process.

Take the time to get a facial and a manicure. Women love good skin and good hands on a man, plus good shoes, good cologne, good teeth, and good style that looks as if you did not try too hard. It is all about grooming with women. Whether you shave your head or grow your hair, get it together. If you have had the same hairstyle since high school, it is time to get contemporary. When you feel good about you, it will help you have more confidence when approaching the woman you want to meet.

Now that you have your image together, you are ready for prime-time TV and closing in on that woman you want. Do one last spot check and determine if your heart is settled. Women do not understand when you put them on hold while you try to make something happen in your career, or begin backpedaling to figure out if you are really ready for a commitment. They always feel that you should be able to juggle more than one thing at a time because they are natural multitaskers. Putting women on hold only makes them more anxious to close the deal because they fear losing you. This puts them in a mode you will not like—one of testing you, issuing ultimatums, getting friends involved in questioning your intentions, and a gamut of unpleasant options. Save yourself the trouble and go for the roll when you know you are ready.

What a Man's Got to Do

When Ruth reached the threshing-room floor, Boaz was in good spirits after celebrating the conclusion of the harvest. He lay down to go to sleep. Softly, she uncovered his feet, lay down, and pulled the corner of the cover over herself. According to the customs of the day, this was literally a marriage proposal. Whoa! *That was bold,* you may be thinking. However, Ruth had the right to do this according to Jewish tradition. The law in Israel stated that if a woman's husband died, his brother or next of kin was to take her as his wife and sire children so the dead man's inheritance would not be lost and his name would continue. Ruth had a right to ask for his covering.

Now do not expect a woman to do your work for you today. We no longer have those traditional guidelines, save one. A real man names his wife, just as Adam did. He makes the declaration of his intentions. Men are supposedly hunters by nature, and your conquest is not complete if you have not been able to experience the hunt in all of its stages.

A woman puts her heart out there, seeking protection from you. Assuming you have not been leading her on, there comes a time when you must step up to the plate to be her "kinsman-redeemer," a man who would redeem her life with his own. It is part of the reason you were created. Your love and care for her should make her a better woman, and vice versa. In a way, marriage is a higher calling, another level of living and giving that truly reflects the heart of God. It is a calling the apostle Paul called a mystery. I call it a journey. It takes a lifetime to master this exciting expedition to the

Personal Confession

I will be cognizant of my role as a man before God and live up to my obligations with integrity.

unknown regions of your very own heart. Marriage becomes the gateway to a higher level of promotion and blessing if you follow God's instructions.

Consider the fact that when law firms and major corporations consider a man for partner or CEO, they check out his family life. When a man runs for office, the country checks out his wife. Why is that? Because we know the atmosphere at home will determine if this man will be capable of doing the job. We know that the woman who shares his bed gets his ear and is a major influence in how he processes his decisions that will ultimately affect us all. God wants to equip you, my brother, for greater success and stability in your life. When is it time to get married? When you can go no further as you are.

The Facts on Women

➤ Women come with the built-in capacity to love a man and cherish him. Because she is wired to respond, be careful of the signals you send out. Do not lead her into a relationship if that is not what you want.

➤ Initially, a man's appearance is just as important to a woman as her appearance is to him. After that, it is what you say and do that bears more weight.

➤ Though a woman likes a man who is exciting, keeping her off-kilter by being emotionally elusive will make her anxious. Be a man of your word.

➤ A woman waits for you to validate her and the relationship by vocalizing your desire to commit. Be sensitive to her heart and let her know where you are in the process.

➤ God created the woman to be a helper to a man. The woman in your life should make you a better man.

Consider This

- Make a list of what is most important to you in a woman. Is there a female friend in your life at present that perhaps you have overlooked?

- In what ways do you feel you are ready for a commitment? What things still scare you when you consider committing?

- Where are you at present? Are you ready for the next level, or are you finishing out your season? What thoughts or feelings have you been experiencing that let you know this?

◄►

*In the Lord, however, a woman is not independent
of man, nor is man independent of woman. For as woman
came from man, so also man is born of woman. But
everything comes from God (1 Corinthians 11:11-12).*

9
A Man of Virtue

Then he [Boaz] said, "Blessed are you of the LORD, my daughter!
For you have shown more kindness at the end than at the
beginning, in that you did not go after young men, whether poor
or rich. And now, my daughter, do not fear. I will do for you all
that you request, for all the people of my town know that you are
a virtuous woman. Now it is true that I am a close relative;
however, there is a relative closer than I. Stay this night, and in the
morning it shall be that if he will perform the duty of a close relative
for you—good; let him do it. But if he does not want to perform the
duty for you, then I will perform the duty for you....Lie down until
morning." So she lay at his feet until morning and she arose
before one could recognize another. Then he said, "Do not let it
be known that the woman came to the threshing floor."

RUTH 3:10-14 NKJV

*W*hat a wonderful conversation between this man and woman that takes place in the darkness of night. Ruth lets Boaz know of her need for him. Soft, vulnerable, and open, she simply makes her request, which must have been fearful for her on some level. After all, he could have said no, even though it was an obligation of the next of kin to marry her. He would be actually taking on a debt by buying back her family plot. But none of this was what crossed the mind of Boaz. Instead, he finds it a privilege that she would approach him in this manner and not go after another man who was younger or richer!

I am sure this surprised her, as one of her concerns had to have been how he would regard her as a Moabite, someone whom most of the Israelites disdained. This avoidance was not just out of personal prejudice, but was actually mandated by God. Here stood two people gazing at one another in wonderment that they had found one another. The true mystery of love is that no matter what our failings and past mistakes, someone will find us lovable because God still loves us.

While many men battle with the fear of rejection, know that women also go through the wringer in this area. They wonder if they are worthy of getting a good man because of their past mistakes, race, life condition, looks, you name it. We all have reasons for a mounting list of insecurities. I want to set you free right now by telling you this: The woman that is for you will not regard your life scars as deterrents. God will shape her heart to accommodate who you are. The things that do not belong there, or that God does not want to subject the woman to, He will work with you to change or remove. But as for the things about you that cannot be reversed or changed, He will make room in the heart of your woman to look beyond your faults and see your needs.

The reason Boaz could be so open to the thought of marrying Ruth was because he was well-acquainted with what it felt like to be an outcast because of background. His own mother was Rahab, the harlot—the woman who had helped the spies from Israel who came to scope out Jericho before the walls fell down. She married one of those spies by the name of Salmon. Together, they gave birth to Boaz. Yes, Boaz knew a thing or two about being ostracized for things you cannot change. It made him a very gracious man who was open to dealing with people according to who they were as individuals.

God has a woman for you no matter what your race or background, no matter what your mistakes have been. Stop apologizing for who you are and begin to embrace your own uniqueness. Know that the things you have been through have made you the valuable person and gift you are today. God can use your experiences to benefit other people, including the woman He has for you. Allow Him to use your pain and your past mistakes. Let God squeeze the lessons out of them and make lemonade to pour out and refresh people around you.

Be Open

Do you have a particular "type" of woman in mind? I would like to give you some food for thought. Remember the king featured in the book of Esther—the one who had the beautiful wife he was so proud of that he called her to show her off to his guests? Well, obviously she was his "type," but she did not do much to enhance who he was in the eyes of his associates and friends because she disgraced him publicly by refusing to come. After getting rid of her and going in search of a new bride, he did not get *his* type; instead, he got the *right* type of woman in Esther. She was beautiful from the inside out. She saved his life at one point, and he saved hers. That is what the right type will do for you.

Here we have another instance where two people should not have been together because of their background. As a matter of fact, Esther had kept hers a secret lest it endanger her chances to become queen. God put these two most unlikely people together in order to form a powerful team that changed history. Because of their marriage, the lives of many Israelites were saved and the holiday of Purim, which is still celebrated today, was established. You will never know the legacy you will leave behind because you chose the right type. Get rid of all your preconceived notions and be open to the endless possibilities of who God wants to put in your life.

Boaz then notes there is an obstacle to him being able to offer Ruth his hand in marriage. I wonder if this was why he had not voiced an interest in her in the first place? There was another relative in line for her hand before him, who was closer in kin than he was. But he would handle the matter! I like a man who takes control, rises to the occasion, and solves the problem. He explained that if the closer relative did not want to do his duty by her, then he would. I really like that—a man of principle! He advised her to lie down and sleep until the morning—in other words, do not worry her pretty little head about a thing. She could rest in the knowledge that her request was already a done deal. Every woman loves a man who can keep his promises. Money is not everything, but a man who keeps his word is.

Ruth did as Boaz instructed her. She lay at his feet until morning. Now you *know* we have to talk about this! It is time to go a little deeper into dealing with the "s" word: sex. She lay at his feet until morning. Nothing happened! As a matter of fact, he woke her up early and sent her on her way because he did not want anyone to see her and begin gossiping about what had not occurred. He became guardian of her reputation, safety, and well-being.

The "S" Word

One of the greatest things a man can do for a woman he really cares about is to care about her spiritual and emotional health. You will not want to compromise her in any way or violate anything that is important to her. I know from my collected data that even a man in the secular world will put off having sex with a woman to preserve her specialness if he thinks she might be "The One." Though most women accept the fact that many men are sexually active inside the church and out, it is disappointing when a man you care for, who supposedly has committed himself to walking according to godly guidelines, pushes you to compromise your purity. Keep in mind, if she cares for you, she is struggling to maintain self-control just as strongly as you are. Help her out and solicit her help when you need it. This area of vulnerability on your part will deepen her love for you when she knows that you are committed to being a godly and chaste man.

I find that most men and women do not stand on principle when it comes to sex because they do not understand the depths of what sex is really all about. For everything in the spiritual realm there is a natural parallel. Sex could be considered a natural parallel to the spiritual act of worship. What is sex? What is worship? It is giving all you have and all you are to the one you love. It is completely yielding yourself to your lover, submitting to one another, praising one another. The woman is literally calling you "lord," which makes you feel powerful. She, on the other hand, receives your strength. This is part of why you crave the sexual experience so strongly. However, it is a dangerous place to be in if that woman does not truly belong to you as your wife. And because the drive to engage in intimacy with this woman is a stronger pull than obedience to God, she can become lord and master over *you*. Deep, isn't it? Small wonder those people who worshiped idols always included sexual orgies as part of their rituals. Even the heathen understood the spiritual implications of sex.

This is why God considers sex outside of marriage, or fornication, to be adultery. He feels you are taking worship away from Him and giving it to an idol. God refuses to share His glory with another or to move aside for idols. God is not into sharing His women or His men until He turns them over to the one whom He has chosen to be the physical extension of His love toward them.

Sex was intended by God to bind two people together. For a woman, it is harder to break it off with someone she has slept with. A man has a much different reaction. If he sleeps with a woman who is not special to him, he has a sense of revulsion and the urgency to get away from her as quickly as possible. He might even leave in the middle of the night. Do you know why? There are several reasons. The first one is because sex goes beyond the physical act to the spiritual. You actually create a soul tie with the other person. You are literally fused to that person.

Both of you have developed a soul tie and, although you deal with it differently, the symptoms are the same whether you choose to be in touch with her or not. To go your separate ways after the sexual exchange is literally a stripping of the soul, like a scarred tree that continues to grow but is marked for life. Long after the separation, phantom pain remains. Even if you had concluded you did not even like the woman, something within you longs for her. Some men are convinced the only way to put out the fire of longing is to return to the same bad situation time and time again. The only thing that happens here is the tie grows stronger. A decision must be made to end the relationship once and for all, while trusting time and the Spirit of God to eventually ease your torment.

So what goes on in a man's mind if he sleeps with a woman for whom he cares deeply? It gets complicated. He is still disappointed on some level because his spirit man knows their interaction was out of spiritual order and he should have done something to preserve the specialness between them. It ruptures the trust factor between them. How much can they trust the other to master self-control in their absence if they could not prove it to one another?

The guilt, if these two people are believers, sometimes pressures them into getting married quickly to avoid having to deal with maintaining their purity. They then find out that sex has clouded issues they had overlooked in each other before they committed their lives to one another. The extreme scenario is they find out they have nothing else in common and the marriage does not last. On the flip side, for those couples who keep falling into sin, recovering for a while, and falling again, many just get tired of the struggle and end up going their separate ways. No one can deal with endless frustration.

Here is the catch-22 for you men. A woman will test a man in the area of sex because of her own need to know that you desire her, but she will be disappointed if you give in to the whole experience. Although she wants a passionate man, she also wants a godly man who is able to exercise discipline. This man loses respect in her eyes because he has stepped off the pedestal and become like every other man. This might feel unfair to the man, who interpreted her moves toward him as wanting to go all the way. Because women are snugglers by nature, they can be satisfied with heavy petting and "fooling around." This only makes a man crazy. Appetizers are a "girlie" thing. Men are main-course people. They would rather avoid the whole meal if they cannot have what they really want. In the end, the pressure makes them fold and abdicate the relationship. A woman might never know or understand why because the man will not vocalize it, but the reason is obvious: Sin can drain a good relationship.

There is also a shame element to breaking up after being intimate. In most translations, when the Bible speaks of someone having God-ordained sex, the word *know* is used: "And Adam knew Eve...and she conceived" (Genesis 4:1 KJV). Whenever it was a union outside of God's perfect design, the Bible says "and he *lie* with her" (a good choice of words), or "he *went unto* her." This knowing spoke of deep intimacy—of someone knowing you in a way that no one else did, of being naked and unashamed, of being completely transparent and hiding nothing from the one you love. Now consider the breakup. This woman walks away carrying pieces of you that you will never recover—your secrets, the very essence of who you are. She can no longer be trusted to guard your heart. What will she do with this delicate information? Will

Personal Confession

I will not compromise myself or my bride before my wedding night. I will take the spiritual lead and seek to preserve our purity for our marriage.

she pass it on to other people or, will she do worse and simply despise you? This is the worst type of rejection. It is irreconcilable to the human spirit. Your soul was not designed to be subjected to such a tearing. It was designed for eternal relationships. Small wonder it takes such a toll on your heart and emotions. No one is supposed to "know" you that well except for your wife.

Next, after putting yourself in the position to be subjected to a woman's power, come the other possibilities to which you open yourself: STD's (sexually transmitted diseases). Every man always thinks it would never happen to him, yet it surprises every victim. It is probably Murphy's favorite law. Then there is the other lifelong consequence: pregnancy. It affects your life just as deeply as it does the woman's. Suddenly your life has been altered forever. Your destiny has taken a sudden turn you did not anticipate. Sacrifices and changes you had not planned to make are now necessary. Life, as you knew it, will be over. Your freedom, so sorely taken for granted, will be gone forever. This is not just a new chapter in your life; it is a whole new book. Children are hard work, and single-parenting is no joke for either parent.

Alternative Measures

Now I hear someone asking, "Well, Michelle, what do I do with my needs? I am suffering! I don't know if I can hold out any longer! If I'm not supposed to do anything, why won't God take the desire away from me?" God is not going to do that because He gave you the desire in the first place. Yes, it is a healthy, God-given desire. Yet you must learn to master your desires. What would happen if you ate whatever you wanted, whenever you felt like it? You would blow up! Everything that feels good to you may not be good for you. There is a time and place for everything. Your attitude toward yourself, as well as your view of what sex is truly all about, must change in order for you to prioritize your standards and keep from walking around like a deprived victim, bereft of joy and fulfillment.

"What about oral sex and masturbation?" you may ask. These are two areas I get questioned about in letters all the time. I always scratch my head, a bit confused by the question. Oral sex is oral *sex*. It is *sex*. I do not care what a past president says. It is still being intimate with the private parts of another person. It is not something you would do in public or with just anybody, although the latest statistics of what is happening in this arena with high school students is frightening. Again, you can contract STD's if you choose to go this route. This is not a shortcut to having your needs met until you can go all the way. This is just another form of the same exercise. You are not fooling anyone—not God, not yourself, not her. Some things are better saved and kept as pleasant surprises within the confines of marriage. Is oral sex wrong? According to my findings in the Song of Songs in the Bible, the answer is no. But outside of marriage, the answer is a resounding yes.

Now on to the M word. Is masturbation wrong? I have no Scripture verse for you on this one. I know that most men are conditioned to believe this is just a "guy" thing. It is something men do. What's the big deal, right? However, let me bring up a couple of thoughts. What happens after you have cleansed your system of sugar and you happen to have one taste? That's right, it makes you want more. Masturbation lights a fire you will not be able to put out. Temporary relief is replaced with greater longing. Unfulfilled longing can lead to depression, obsession, and oppression, which can cause you to reach a breaking point and do something rash. The other part of this equation is you are setting yourself up for difficulty when you do finally get a mate. How can someone please you when you have learned to please yourself? Unless you are highly communicative and demonstrative, she will never be able to duplicate what you have been doing, which could lead to frustration and unfulfillment. Your level of delight and satisfaction would have been easier to reach and maintain minus the self-experimentation.

Taking Control

What is a man to do to handle hormones on the prowl within his body? Redirect your passion, energy, and attention. First, let's deal with your mind. It all starts there. If sex is all you think about, guess what? Your body will follow the cues from your mind. I always cite the story in 2 Samuel chapter 13, of Amnon and Tamar, to give an extreme example of this. Amnon, King David's son, obsesses over his stepsister Tamar, believing himself to be deeply "in love" with her. Actually, he was "in lust" with her. You have to know the difference. Even women can be guilty of this. If the woman in your life is more interested in exploring your body than in investigating your mind and personality, or vice versa, get a clue. If your conversations with her are always superficial, never going to a deeper level, yet you are getting closer physically and it is all about incredible chemistry, pay attention. You might be knee-deep in self-deception. It got to the point where Amnon became sick, he was so overwhelmed with his constant longing for Tamar. It consumed his every thought. When he finally got Tamar alone in his presence, he could no longer contain himself and he raped her. His feelings quickly turned to disgust and hatred, and he basically dumped her! And you thought this only happened in our modern day.

What got him to the point of no return? It was his refusal to get a grip on his thought life. This is difficult in today's culture where we are assaulted with sexual innuendos that permeate everything from a commercial about instant rice, to cars, to the right clothing to wear. Music is so sensual. If it is not the groove that gets you going, it is the lyrics and their explicit suggestions. What does that mean for you? You must set your own boundaries based on your personal weaknesses. If music gets your thoughts going down the wrong path, then you must become the sentry over your ears and what you allow in.

Job, in the book of Job, said he would set no evil thing before his eyes. He knew what he saw fed his mind images that could result in the wrong actions. Avoid movies or visual images that tickle your fancy as well as your senses. Conversations could also be added to the list. Talk stimulates our imaginations, so reel in your words. Do not start fires you cannot extinguish. You must exercise control over your thoughts and your imagination. Avert your attention to something else that feeds your spirit or gets you stimulated in other ways: a worthwhile project or another area of interest you have been putting on hold. Use all that energy to produce something beneficial for your life and for people around you.

People laugh when I tell them to find a physical activity to get involved in. That could be working out, walking, playing tennis, whatever exercise you like to do. A tired body is a satisfied body. The energy in your body has to have an outlet. This is important even if you are married and are free to express yourself sexually. It is amazing to me how many married people are not having sex or are not even interested! It stands to reason that, if this is the case, sex is highly overrated in the minds of those who have to wait to indulge. But while you are waiting, get in shape so you have a healthy body that you will not be ashamed to present to your marriage partner. Sex can be wonderful when you are healthy, married, and whole in the area of intimacy.

Last, but not least, build up your spirit so it becomes stronger than your flesh. Whatever you feed the most will become the strongest. Center yourself in the Word of God and worship Him. Reel in your thoughts and place them in obedience to Christ. After reading the Bible and having a great time with God before going to bed, your sleep will be sweet and uninterrupted by thoughts of things you cannot do anything about.

Getting on the Right Track

Why is the area of sexual purity so important for you to master? Because how you deal with this part of your interaction with the woman of your dreams will set the course of your relationship and affect your marriage. If you do things God's way, you will not go to the marriage bed with issues that stop you from enjoying yourself. On the other hand, premarital sex can stop you from getting to the altar. Keep in mind that a good woman wants a good man. She wants you to preserve your integrity and image in her eyes if you are the one she wants to marry. This is one of the greatest tests of leadership she will want you to pass. She wants you to be like Boaz, who wanted to preserve the integrity of Ruth privately and publicly. This is what a man will do when he truly loves a woman and cares about what is important to her. You should take just as much responsibility as she does when it comes to maintaining your sexual purity, because it definitely takes two to tango!

Personal Confession

I will purpose to guard my heart, as well as my body, and stay focused on the rewards of purity versus its immediate sacrifices.

It's All in the Family

Now let's move on to see how Boaz and Ruth's relationship was clinched. I like the next move Boaz made, described in verse 15 of chapter 3. He loaded her down with a large portion of barley, being cognizant of which needs he could fill in her life immediately. You can also hear the difference in his intent toward her when he says, "Do not go empty-handed to your mother-in-law." He now cares what Naomi thinks because of the relationship he hopes to have with Ruth. Men, I know you do not like this part, but you are going to have to deal with her family. Anything that is precious to her should be precious to you. She will be just as nervous about meeting and impressing your family as you are about hers. Women generally are ready to introduce the man to their family earlier than the man is ready to introduce her to his, but do not get shaky when it comes up.

If you are not ready, speak up and let her know you do not feel you are at that level in your relationship yet. Many women have grown wiser over the years and are a little more careful about introducing men to their families. Unless they feel he is going to be around, they usually do not go there. If you are interested in being with this woman, it behooves you to go and meet her family. The truth of the matter is, you are not just marrying one person. You are marrying into a family.

Some men would like to think they are not marrying the other person's family, but indeed they are. First of all, her mother is going to give you big hints on your wife-to-be. This is the woman who has been a role model of womanhood for her. She will be a lot like her mother now, and even more so in the years to come. Because Christ can transform us, your woman might be the opposite of her mother if there are a lot of things she does not like about her. You have to be careful to note if your woman has released her mother and accepted her as she is with love. Or is she bitter? If she is bitter, she can become bound to her mother in the spirit and actually end up subconsciously harboring her mother's same attitudes and manifesting them in different ways. For example, let's say her mother was an alcoholic. She now despises alcohol and the effect alcoholism had on her mother because it caused her mother to be abusive to her father, herself, and the other children. Now your woman does not touch a drop of liquor, but she has an addictive nature. She indulges it in other areas that she does not believe are wrong, and from time to time you feel she can be verbally abusive. It behooves you to observe your woman's family and not discard what you see.

Let's talk about family dynamics for a moment. When it comes to your woman and your family, observe how she treats them and interacts with them. Is she comfortable with them? How does your family respond to her, especially your mother? If a mother is not present, then gather information from the other significant female relatives or friends you have. Women know other women and will let you know exactly what type of woman she is without even blinking. They will definitely tell you if she is worthy of your time. If you have children from a previous relationship, what is her interest level in those children? How does she interact with them? Her behavior will let you know just how much she loves you by her ability to love your children. Anything that is a part of you, she will openly embrace and love. The family encounter can definitely lift and separate truth from fiction in a relationship. At the right time, it is important to have other people who are more objective than yourself check her out.

We know that Naomi thought highly of Boaz and recommended him to Ruth, so he already had high points. He was well thought of in the community and among his own workers. All the right foundational traits were in place, and then he tops them off by having special regard not only for Ruth, but also for the only family she had. He sends her away full. He was full as well because he was energized by the fact he was about to claim the hand of a good woman who held him in high regard. This is what people do when they love one another and are right for one another. Both of you should be adding to one another's life, not subtracting from one another and from where you were in life before the other person arrived on the scene. The woman in your life should multiply the fruit in your life, not divide your focus and make you uncertain of the things you once held dear. She should make you full. She should be a woman you are not ashamed to present to the world, as well as to your inner circle. Now that you are sure she is "The One," you have work to do.

Boaz told Ruth he would take care of what needed to be done in order to secure her future. This is a man's job. A real man knows this. And a real woman knows that a real man will do what he has to do to get what he wants. This will be a test of how you take the lead and follow through. This will solidify in her mind if she can trust you and respect you enough to submit to you. She will gauge how much of the relationship and daily running of your lives together she will have to be responsible for. This is where you will set the course for your marriage. Once she feels nervous that you "don't take care of business," she will decide she has to do it for you. If you plan to be in charge at your house, you better lay the foundation now. If you are allowing her to make all the decisions because you think this makes her happy, think again. Later, you will be unhappy. Actually, so will she, because a woman wants a man who will step up to the plate and hit a home run for the team. The less you take charge, the less she will respect you. Eventually she will no longer be attracted to you. Therefore, in order to maintain the romance factor in your relationship, you must lovingly, but firmly, take the lead. So plan your work and work your plan, men.

 The Facts on Women

➤ A woman is a complex being. Take the time necessary to allow all the layers of her to unfold before drawing conclusions.

➤ In courtship, women test men in the area of sex because they need the assurance they are desirable to you, not because they want to consummate the act.

➤ Women are disappointed when men who claim to have a relationship with God compromise their stand on purity.

➤ A woman looks to a man to take the lead. She will willingly follow if he walks in wisdom.

Consider This

- Where are you when it comes to maintaining your purity? What are your struggles? What are some working solutions for you?

- Have you reconciled any family issues you have? In what areas do you need healing in order to have more healthy interactions with your loved ones and with your bride?

- What does your picture of home life look like? What is the part you must play in order to capture that vision?

◄►

Therefore, I urge you, brothers, in view of God's mercy, to offer your bodies as living sacrifices, holy and pleasing to God—which is your spiritual worship (Romans 12:1).

10

Where the Rubber Hits the Road

> Then Boaz said, "On the day you buy the land from
> Naomi and from Ruth the Moabitess, you acquire the dead man's
> widow, in order to maintain the name of the dead with
> his property." At this, the kinsman-redeemer said,
> "Then I cannot redeem it because I might endanger
> my own estate. You redeem it yourself. I cannot do it."
>
> RUTH 4:5-6

Once his mind was made up to claim the hand of Ruth, Boaz had his own little plan of how to get her hand. Do you have a plan for your relationship? I am constantly amazed at the length of time that goes into some courtships. Couples have been together for six or eight years and still do not know when they are getting married. What is *that* about? How does this happen? All of a sudden there is a breakup, and one of the parties goes off and marries someone else in a matter of months. What was the difference between the relationships? One had a plan, and the other one did not. Perhaps one or both parties made far too many comforts reserved for marriage before the committment had been made, thus killing the urgency to seal the deal.

Many years ago, I met the man of my dreams. Unfortunately, he lived on an island. He wanted to marry me, and everything within me was in conflict. Could I leave my way of life in the States and live on an island? I had lived there as a child, but this was the grown-up world now. I had my own thoughts, hopes, and dreams and did not see them coming to pass on this island. He sensed my ambivalence and gave me some time to sort out my thoughts and decide what I was going to do. I kind of dragged my feet on the entire issue, not really willing to give him up, but not willing to pay the price to keep him. Well, you guessed it. He called it a day and within months he was married to someone else. I was shocked, even though I should not have been. He had a plan. He wanted to be married. He met someone else who wanted to be married and was willing to do what she had to do in order to make it happen. She moved from another island to be with him.

Men, this is big for you. Although I am addressing having a plan, I am also talking about paying the price for what you want. She has to be willing to pay the price and so do you. She must be willing to follow you, to be with you where you are. In the Old Testament this was a mandate Abraham gave his servant Eliezer when he sent him to get a bride for Isaac. Not only was she to be from among Abraham's people, but she also had to be willing to forsake her family and *move to where Isaac was*. Otherwise, Eliezer was to leave her there. Why is this important? Because it affects your sense of manhood.

You are called to lead, not follow. Anytime you compromise on this, you will grow resentful because you will be going against the grain of who you are as a man. If a woman's location or career is too important to her and causes her to have reservations about being where you are, back up. She is already making a loud statement about her priorities. Both people in the relationship are called to pay a price for being together. It is a matter of give-and-take, but there is also a spiritual order to things. Unless God has told you to move, stay put and allow

Him to not only move her, but move her heart if she is the one for you.

Boaz was a man with a plan. He knew exactly how to negotiate the delicate matter of gaining the hand of Ruth. First, he went to find the kinsman-redeemer who really had first rights to marrying Ruth. When Boaz found him, in the presence of witnesses he broached the matter. He informed the relative that Naomi had returned from Moab and sold the property belonging to her husband. It was his option to buy the land back to keep it in the family. Of course, the man wanted the land. He would stand to gain a lot from it. He could plant crops on it, earn back the money used to purchase it in no time, and move on to greater profits. It was not difficult to see what he would get out of the deal. Ah, but when Boaz brought up the fact that Ruth would have to come with the land, the relative changed his tune. He was not interested in adding Ruth to his list of responsibilities. It could cause problems for him and affect his inheritance. No, that was too high a price to pay. He was willing to pass on the land and what he could gain from it in order to avoid having to take care of Ruth.

The Value of Love

Remember the story of the pearl of great price? The man sold all he had in order to find it. The same has to be true in love at some point. You have to be willing to give your all, your everything. This is scary for a man, I know. But the manliest man of all, that romantic warrior, Jesus, laid down His life for His bride. In the Upper Room, He prayed and told the Father His greatest longing was for His disciples to be where He was and to see Him as He truly was in glory (John 17:24).

Part of getting your bride to see you as you are is to allow her to see your heart through what you are willing to do for her. She wants to know you consider her worth the price of your freedom and all you hold dear: your future, your inheritance, your security, your everything. She would like a glimpse of your future together and what your plans are. The Lord says to His people, "For I know the plans I have for you" (Jeremiah 29:11). Jesus said to His bride, "I am going to prepare a place for you" (John 14:2). He has plans for us. This is important to a woman for her peace of mind. Ruth was not stressed because Boaz had a decisive plan of action that he vowed to carry out. He did not tell her all the details, but he did not have to because he had already proven himself to be a man who made things happen. She was free to marry him without reservation because he walked the walk.

What type of things does a woman consider before releasing her hand in marriage to you? What things should you consider before you ask for her hand? The first things, after feelings, are more practical matters. This is where your habits should come under scrutiny. Lots of questions should be asked. Though Ruth and Boaz did not have marriage counseling per se, I highly suggest that couples take the time to talk everything out with an objective party before the wedding. Get on the same page or close the book before it costs you more than you have or want to pay.

First on the checklist is the area of finances. Your present habits, collectively, will tell you a lot about your future. How are your finances and hers? How do you both spend your money? Do you have any savings or investments? Are you always putting out fires with your bills? Do you live from paycheck to paycheck? How many credit cards do you have? Are they all at their limit? Get it together. No one wants to inherit debt. You do not, and I am sure she does not. The first thing Ruth's next of kin said was he did not want to marry her because it would affect his estate.

The next area on the checklist is personal habits: reliability, sensitivity, communication, respect, honesty, supportiveness. How do you resolve conflict? How do you respond to pressure? How do you handle anger? Where do you see yourselves in five or ten years? What are your thoughts on child-rearing? Do you feel called to any specific ministry, charity, or cause? What are your passions? What is your love language? Do you have an understanding of one another in this area? What does a pleasant day as a couple look like? It is time to lay all the cards and expectations on the table. The fewer surprises and misconceptions you have to work through after you say "I do," the better. You will have a whole new set of adjustments to make as it is!

Make your first plan of action the decision to always communicate—no matter what. I recall a friend of mine telling me that she told her husband before they got married that if he ever felt tempted by another woman, she wanted him to tell her. That way they could walk through the situation together. She could forgive him for being tempted. But if he kept it a secret and fell into adultery and she found out, she would have a hard time forgiving him and staying married to him. They have kept this vow to the present day, walking in transparency with one another without incident. Relationships thrive when openness is present. When a couple starts withholding information, the gap between them widens to the point where you have two strangers living under the same roof. The marriage has nowhere to go because the noncommunication chasm eventually seems too wide to cross. Because a man's approval is very important and validating to a woman, it makes her feel safe to communicate her heart with you—the good, the bad, and the ugly—without the fear of later repercussions.

Taking Care of You and Yours

When I consider the list of traits that Bathsheba related to her son Solomon about the type of woman he should look for as a life partner in Proverbs 31, not only does she stress how this woman would take care of him, but also how she took care of herself and other people. This detailed description was a crystal-clear picture of what her spirit and her heart really looked like. A woman can be on good behavior for only so long before the real person begins to surface in her attitude toward herself, as well as toward other people. You see, when Boaz saw Ruth, it was not just her outer beauty that struck him, but her inner beauty as well. There were lots of things about her that were apparent to him that were a major plus. So while you are checking out the outer stuff, take one more look at the inward parts.

Ruth was resourceful. She was not a victim of her circumstances, but a victor in spite of them. Though she was self-sufficient, she was not prideful. She was able to accept help graciously. A man would not have to wonder if she could handle life if something happened to him and he was not able to be there for her and his family. She would be a survivor and able to take care of their family. She had what it took to be his partner, helping to carry the load of life between them. Her spirit reflected that she had her life in order. Whatever she could not handle was secure in the hands of God. These traits should signal to you that life with her will not be one emergency after the other. Together, you will be able to implement plans for the future and see them through to fruition.

Personal Confession

I will purpose to read the book before I buy it for the cover.

This brings me to my second point: wisdom. A man needs a woman in his life who brings something to the relationship intellectually. He needs a thinking partner, not a bossy partner, not one who knows everything and is never wrong, not one who always talks and never listens. He needs a thinking woman with grace. He needs someone he can plan his life with and receive wise counsel from during the times when he is not quite sure which way to go. Watch how she plans her life and functions daily, how she rationalizes situations that may be trying or difficult. A woman can make or break a man with her attitude and her counsel. Opt for a woman who adds to your bank of wisdom and supports you to higher levels in your life.

Make sure you marry a woman you can talk to. I find it interesting that in most cases where a husband runs off with another woman, it is because he finds her to be a more stimulating partner not just sexually, but mentally as well. He feels he has finally met his equal—someone he can really talk to, someone who understands him, respects his ideas, and thinks he is wonderful, someone who not only loves him, but *serves* him.

And yes, I, a woman, brought up the word *serve*. You are called to serve her and she is called to serve you. When a woman encounters a servant/leader man, it is over—she will become putty in your hands. I can tell you the inside scoop that not many men know how to treat a woman these days. So when we meet one who does, we are all over him! I will expound on this a little later. If you are both serving one another, both of your needs are being met. Do not attach yourself to an uncooperative woman and blame God for it later. Remember, He gives you the gift of choice. You do not want a woman who is always questioning you, coming up with a way to do the task better, or overlooking the obvious needs that you have. It can only get uglier after marriage. I recall being at the home of a friend of mine who told her husband, with me standing there, that he should just do what she said because obviously she was smarter than he was! I was mortified and so was he. I left wondering how much longer that marriage would last.

Now is the time to see if you feel listened to and understood, if your word is respected and you are honored. Observe if she is able to praise you and celebrate who you are and what you do. Make sure she does not seek her own way in the relationship. Instead, she should try to find a place of agreement so that both of your needs are met. She is strong but soft at the same time because she has mastered the art of being a woman.

Creating an Oasis

How about her homemaking skills? When you enter her home, do you like the way you feel? After marriage, you will be living in the environment she sets, for the most part. Your house should be a place you want to come home to. Does she have a domestic bone in her body, or does she just live at her house? Can she cook? Does it feel like a real woman lives there, or does it feel like a temporary holding station? I believe part of the reason that many single women are overwhelmed with feeling as if their life is not complete without a man is because they have done nothing to their environment to give them a sense of completion. The woman you are looking for loves the space she lives in. She is able to rejoice about the wonderful life she is living, while being able to celebrate the wonderful addition of you to a blessed life that was already rich. That takes the pressure off of you to supply *all* of her happiness.

Setting Your House in Order

Ah, but what about you, my brother? It would be unfair for this woman to be so together and not be able to receive as great a package. Now I will give you your personal checklist. For a more detailed guide, please see my book *In Search of the Proverbs 31 Man* (WaterBrook, 2003). Taking care of business, self, and home, while nurturing a spirit that is a rich reservoir for a woman to draw from, puts you in line to be highly esteemed above other men. Ask yourself the same questions I asked you to consider as you observe the woman in your life. Remember the song that said, "No romance without finance…gotta have a j-o-b if you wanna be with me"? Make sure you are prepared to take a bride home. Prepare a house for her, or at least have the means to get one together.

Jesus, the ultimate Bridegroom, saw what He wanted, fought for it, won it, and then moved on to prepare a place for His hard-won bride. Jesus knows how to treat a woman. He loved His bride so much that He gave everything He had for her—heart, mind, body, and soul—His very life. He washed her. He covered her failings. He fought her enemies. He constantly reassured her of His love and will not leave her comfortless. He is presently preparing a house for her, as well as a wedding feast to celebrate her arrival. Now, that is a man! That is what I am talking about. Every man with a plan knows how to win a woman.

Men, you need to rediscover the art of conversation. Women are moved by what they hear much more than by what they see. The constant complaint I hear is that men no longer have a conversation worthy of listening to. The pursuit, as well as courtship, are in a state of flux. Jesus was charismatic, had a way with words and a sense of humor, and had that certain X factor that drew devoted women to His side. Men, get creative! Ideas abound from simple to lavish on how to win the heart of a woman.

Not too long ago, on the television show that I cohost, we reenacted "The Dating Game." One of my questions to the bachelors was, "You have 24 hours to win my heart. You have no restrictions, and money is no object. How will we spend our time together?" The answers were lame! The best answer was, "We would fly to New York for dinner and catch a show." That is nice, but if you are talking to a woman who travels all the time, that is no biggie. She has already been there, done that. Later, I was talking to a male friend of mine, and I asked him what his answer would have been. He said, "I would hire the Concorde and fly us to the south of France, where I would have dinner and some musicians waiting on a private stretch of the seaside. We would eat, stroll, and watch the sun go down. Then we would get back on the Concorde and fly to an island on the other side of the world where the sun was coming up so we could start the day all over again and do whatever you wanted to do!" Wow! That blew me away. The moral of the story: Use your imagination. A good woman is moved by the fact that you went outside the box and got creative.

I will give you another example. A man who was in pursuit of me went on a mission trip to Africa. The day after he arrived, he called me from a remote village on a satellite phone he had managed to borrow from someone. He had rounded up a group of the village children with their drums and had them serenade me over the phone. I have to tell you, I was hooked after that. With women, it is the little things that count. Go for it! The sky is the limit.

Taking care of a woman is as simple as taking care of yourself. Open the door for her. Pull out the chair. Compliment her. Help her when she seems to be in a quandary. Offer help before she has to ask. Servant/leader men are so sexy! I was at a church recently and, before I went up to speak, the men's Bible study group came to pray for me. I was ready to move to that city and church. Again, it is the little things. Ask your women friends the types of things men have done that have touched their hearts.

I recall a male friend of mine accompanying me on a ministry trip because I had someone stalking me. On this trip, he took such good care of me that I had to pray a special prayer and ask God for an older clone of him. He took care of every aspect of my trip, from making sure I had my airline ticket (which I had left in the seat at the airport—he noticed when I got up and left it) to making sure I had something to eat when I fell asleep on the plane. He ordered my food at a restaurant when the waiter came while I was away from the

Personal Confession

I will wait until I am completely willing to serve, as well as lead my bride, before I commit to the covenant of marriage.

table, and prayed for me before I spoke. In addition he spent his time helping me with my ministry products, joining me in a question/answer period with the audience, and giving a man's perspective on the subject of my speech. He protected me and eased my fears on what could have been a scary trip. I felt safe with him and could not stop voicing my appreciation for his friendship and his care. I am not high-maintenance, in case you were wondering. I am just a little scattered from time to time. For me, what he did was huge, though it might seem insignificant to you. It was the little things. If he were ten years older, I would marry him! (I have nothing against younger men, but I do have a limit.)

All I am saying is that the lover anticipates the needs of the beloved from the smallest to the greatest and makes sure those needs are met. That is the model for courtship and marriage as set by Christ Himself. It is a small price to pay for the love you want to receive in return. And believe me, if you do what you are supposed to do, the return will be automatic.

Some men are willing to pay the price, some are not. Based on what you perceive her value to be, the determination will be made to take the plunge or not. Only you will be able to decide the outcome of that question. As the song goes, "A real man knows a real woman when he sees her." It takes a real man to recognize a woman's worth and be willing to pay the price. Just know that if you have done all your homework, nothing is keeping you from going to the next level but you.

 The Facts on Women

➤ Every woman wants a man to woo her, pursue her, and win her hand. It speaks volumes about her value in his eyes.

➤ It is the little things that a man says and does that turn a woman's heart toward him. Conversation with no action drives her away.

➤ When a man makes a woman feel safe, he wins her devotion.

➤ When a woman is ready for marriage, she begins to nest by becoming very focused on making her house a home.

Consider This

- What things are missing from your checklist when you consider the woman in your life? Are they realistic desires or not? Are any of them negotiable?

- What areas do you need to work on in how you relate to a significant woman in your life?

- What little things can you do for the woman in your life based on things she has mentioned in the past?

- Do you think the price we are called to pay for love is reasonable? What have you not been willing to do before? What are you willing to do now?

Many a man claims to have unfailing love,
but a faithful man who can find? (Proverbs 20:6).

11

Paying the Cost to Be the Boss

And Boaz said to the elders and all the people, "You are witnesses
this day that I have bought all that was Elimelech's, and all that was
Chilion's and Mahlon's, from the hand of Naomi. Moreover, Ruth
the Moabitess, the widow of Mahlon, I have acquired as my wife."

RUTH 4:9-10 NKJV

This is called stepping up to the plate and doing what has to
be done, no matter what the cost. One man considered the cost
of marrying Ruth and decided it was too high for him. If he
married her, and she had sons, they would be entitled to inher-
iting the land he had purchased in order to gain her hand. This
would cost the children he already had because he would be
taking money that had been stored up for them to purchase the
land from Naomi. He would have to sacrifice one thing in order
to gain another with the possibility of no return. There were
also concerns about adding another woman to his household.
And, last but not least, Ruth was actually a liability because she
came adding nothing. She did not have a dowry. Ruth was an
expensive woman!

When a man truly loves and wants a woman, no price is too
high. He will give his all to acquire his pearl of great price. Boaz
is the prototype of a man who earns a woman's love and respect

by laying his all on the line. Jesus did it for His collective bride, the church, and He has placed that same spirit in the heart of every real man who understands his position in the love relationship. Consider this fact: Ruth was nowhere around when this transaction or agreement took place. He was quite capable of handling the matter on his own. He did not need Ruth's help figuring out what to do. He knew what he wanted and determined what he had to do to get it.

Men, let ask you: How are you in the area of problem-solving, as well as follow-through? How do you interact with people? How do you handle stress? Are you able to calmly gather the facts and make rational and wise decisions under pressure? Or do you explode, fall apart, or become paralyzed? This is important. Why? Because your weaknesses will be a part of the foundation for everything else that goes on in your home. If your wife and children do not feel secure under your leadership, you will have chaos. You will end up with a rebellious wife, and children who disregard your instruction and go their own way.

Count the cost of your marriage before you commit. There is a funny thing about the price versus the cost of some things we buy. The price is the amount set in stone, but the cost is what we pay for upkeep for the life of our ownership. I recently purchased a home. Believe me, the price of the place is entirely different from the cost of home ownership. There is always something else to fix or buy in order to make the home comfortable for other people, as well as myself. If I had foreseen all of the costs up front, I might not have purchased it. But if I look at the long-term investment, it will be well worth it. Every wise man considers what he is getting himself into and makes a decision based on his findings. Sometimes something is worth the investment and sacrifice, and sometimes it is a losing proposition. You must be honest in your assessment for the sake of everyone involved.

I have a friend who was worried about how materialistic his beautiful bride was, but brushed his issues away, even after calling off the wedding once in the midst of his reservations. It was a big mistake. They did not make it. I have observed many couples who struggled with their decision and called off the wedding. Then, because of the pressure from peers and family, because the hall had already been paid for, because the invitations had already been sent, they decided to "go through with it." Those words echo in my spirit. The minute anyone says they need to just "go through with it," or "get on with it," or "get it over with," there is trouble. Why no one ever rationalizes that the cost of cancellation before a wedding is far less than the cost of a divorce spiritually and financially after the wedding eludes me.

The first spiritual rule of conduct when moving forward with any decision in life is this: when in doubt, do not do it. Take that unsettled feeling as a cue from the Holy Spirit that either this is not the move to make, or it is not the time to make it. Do not move forward unless you have a complete release and peace in your soul about your decision. The only pressure to which you should ever give in is that of the voice of the Lord speaking to your inner man.

The Nature of a Woman

Yes, consider the ways of your woman and heed the voice that whispers truth in your hidden man. Boaz considered and heeded and was on his way to take care of the matter. He told Ruth to go home and wait until he was finished. Her response cemented his commitment to marry her. She did what he said. Isn't that refreshing? She did not ask questions. She simply trusted him and released him to do what a man does. Observe the nature of the woman before you. I will probably get in trouble with my sisters for sharing the following inside information with you, but I feel I must if I truly want to invest in your life. It is amazing to me how many men still have not figured out women and their ways. I am going to help you out, and hopefully save you a lot of wasted time and trouble in the long run.

When it comes to women, there are basically four types. First, there is the Seductress. She has nothing to offer, so she uses what she has to get what she wants from you. She is bold and dresses seductively. If she says she is a Christian, she will use the guise of being demure for the sake of appearance. She knows how to say all the right things to swell your ego without you suspecting that is what she is doing. She knows how to touch you and then back off to add some spice to the game. For her it is just a game. She takes her time and does the dance. She knows how to keep you just a little off balance until she makes you crazy. Then she raises the stakes for spending time in her presence. By then, the hunter in you has been sucked into believing (though you suspect you are getting played) you must now capture the prize. Instead, the tables are turned, and the hunter gets captured by the game. She smells good, she looks good, and there is something mysterious about her that makes you desire to know more. She knows just the right move to make that will leave something on your mind when your time with her is about to be over. She casts her line, and then reels you in. She distracts you to no end. She focuses on sensual plea-sure, rather than feeding your soul, until the voice of your flesh drowns out the small whisper of the Spirit.

Every time your ego is challenged to claim her, she makes sure you give her a gift to prove your adoration. *Do you have any money? Could you help me with this or that? Why don't we go away this weekend? I'll make the arrangements, and then you can pay for it. Oh, I had an emergency, and now I don't have the money to pay my rent!* This woman will always need something from you: your time, your money, your body, your mind. Yes, it is true: Once she gets your body, she will have your mind. She has had practice. She knows what to do, and convinces you that you are the only one. Think again. The Seductress will drain your spirit, your strength, and leave you for dead after you are com-pletely tapped out.

On her way out of the relationship, this woman will make sure to tell you it was all your fault! And in a way, it is. You should have seen it coming. She will always make you her victim. Your friends waved red flags, but you were too blinded by all her flattery and seduction to see them. You might even lose a couple friends in the process. Avoid this woman at all costs. She is the one who will boldly stare at you from across the room, but never approach, drawing you to herself with her silent language. Oh yes, she will let you pursue, because she has mastered the art of making men believe that everything they do for her is their idea. She will convince you that it is all about you when it is really all about her.

Next is the Manager. This woman is also dangerous. You might not notice at the start that something is wrong. Based on where you are emotionally and your relationship with your mother, you might miss the cues on this one. If your mother was controlling, she might feel safe and normal to you. This woman is aggressive, decisive, and yes, she will come after you. She will start a relationship and pull you through it before you know you want to be in one. She has convincing conversation, can be incredibly charming, and she is more than willing to help you make up your mind about anything you are not sure of.

The Manager is always sure of what she wants and is determined to have it her way. She has no praise for her man—only criticism to keep him unsure of himself and dependent on her. She is not above manipulation; it is her main calling card. She will pull your string and lead you along the path of her agenda so smoothly that you will not even know it until you wake up to check out the scenery. If you decide you do not want to cooperate, that is when things get ugly. Anything that works will be enforced at that moment: vocal digs that cause you to question yourself, insults to put you in your place, quiet spells of sulking, tears, playing the misunderstood victim in order to make you give in to her wishes, or just an all-out tantrum to put you on the defensive so she can further accuse you of not caring! She will do whatever she has decided will make you cave in, based on what she has observed of your temperament. Oh, did I tell you she is usually a great judge of character? Of course she is, because she has to figure out how to get everyone to bow to her will.

She, like Jezebel in the Bible (who challenged her husband and practically called him a wimp by asking him, "Are you a king or not?"), will wear you down until you completely abdicate your post as leader. She will rationalize that she has to take over because you are passive or indecisive, and she will convince other people in your circle that you are weak as well. The bad thing about the Manager is, not only will she break your spirit, she will spawn other seeds of rebellion in your home. Your children will mirror her behavior in disastrous relationships of their own later in life. She is oblivious to everyone else's comfort in the pursuit of her own. She will never submit. She will emasculate you and leave you in ruins. And yes, this woman will blame you, too. The aftermath of her bad decisions will be all your fault because you never rose to the occasion and made a decision.

You see men married to these women everywhere. These men are the silent sufferers who have learned to say, "Yes, dear" automatically. When you look in his eyes, you know he has vacated the premises and retreated to his own private world where she cannot reach him, leaving her free to spew her venom without him noticing or caring. Otherwise, he chooses more dangerous escapes: affairs, drugs, pornography, alcoholism, or workaholism. The end result is not good. He will be an empty shell of a man who missed out on fulfilling his destiny because he allowed a woman to take over and run him into the ground. How will you recognize her? She will approach you, and everyone in her entourage is driven by her orders.

Then there is the Gleaner. She is a type of Ruth: steady, soft, serene, yet strong. She is very much a woman. She has had some knocks in life, been through a few things, but they have all contributed to the grace she now carries. Highly thought of by all who know her, she does not insist on carving out her own space. She waits to be invited. She is slow and steady, making no assumptions or quick judgments, just accepting the attention she gets without pressing for more. You might even wonder if she really likes you. She does, but she also believes in allowing a man to be a man. Not wasting her heart or her time, she focuses on what she can control and leaves the rest to fall in place.

She is in no hurry, which will mystify you, but it is not because she is playing games. Quite the contrary. Everything she does is exercised after much thought. She counts the cost of what she says and does before proceeding forward. She is careful with her heart, as well as with the hearts of other people. Disappointments have tempered her, though she is not bitter. Definitely better for her experiences, she has learned the value of patience and waiting on God. She might not seem exciting, but do not let her quiet demeanor fool you. Still waters run deep. She reserves excitement for the right moments. This is a woman who has known enough pain to appreciate joy, enough loss to embrace love passionately. She does not cling too tightly because losses have taught her to wear life and the things she acquires loosely.

This woman has a lot to give from a wealth of experiences and wisdom acquired along the way. She is a woman who will make you feel good and look good. She is a helpmeet for you, one who will walk beside you, submit to you, encourage you, and make you a better man. You will want to be one for her. Because of her spirit, she will bring wealth to your house on several levels: emotionally, spiritually, physically, and perhaps even financially. You will finally be free to focus on your calling. She will create an atmosphere in your home that breeds peace, fulfillment, and success. This is the one your mother will like, which might cause you to initially rebel. But if you spend a season in her presence, you will decide she is well worth the investment of your heart. The part that will be unsettling for you, if you have been through major upheavals with other women before, is there will be no more drama. What *will* you do with all those good feelings?

And lastly, there is the Secret Star. This is the one you might not notice right away because she is an unfolding flower. Others will see her before you do. People may even say she is perfect for you. She is beautiful, inside and out, but perhaps she just does not strike you one way or the other. Until you reach the season in your own life when you get over all the external flash and look for something deeper, this star waits to be chosen. Like a diamond waiting for the right setting, she simply shines where she is. She could be a Seductress if she wanted to, but chooses not to manipulate men with her beauty. There is almost an innocence to her that is unaware of how beautiful she is, which makes her all the more attractive. She may be a queen in her own right, but would never flaunt it. She walks in favor with God and man, and good fortune follows her.

Once you have chosen her, she has your back. This woman is a prayer warrior, yielded to her husband and God. She will be your friend and your confidante. She will know how to feed your spirit and your body. Your needs will be placed above her own. She is just as passionate about the needs of people outside her home as she is about her family. She has a charitable heart. She is smart, but she does not flaunt her knowledge. She knows how to place the ball in her husband's court and allow him to be king of his domain. She chooses her battles and considers her timing when dealing with sensitive matters. She is the type of woman a man thanks God for. She is a series of pleasant sur-prises because dimensions of her continue to unfold throughout your journey together. She could be summed up as everything you want and everything you need. Your heart is safe in her hands because she is totally submitted to God's hands. She will help you and not hinder you all the days of your life.

On that note, I vote for the Gleaner and the Secret Star! Some of you are still stuck on the Seductress, I know. Unfortu-nately, most men have been convinced you cannot have excitement in love without a little trash mixed in. Decent women have a hard time capturing a man's attention because they might not have rehearsed all the silky lines and moves that send your blood rushing. Well, every woman cannot be Jessica Rabbit who purred, "I'm not bad. I'm just drawn that way." When watching the adult cartoon *Who Framed Roger Rabbit?* it became quite evident what every man's fantasy looks like. For the most part, good women are solid. They are real women with real passions, and lots of love to give. A real man knows how to influence a woman into becoming his fantasy woman. So do not pass up a good woman while you are looking for an imaginary one. This will take some time to sink in—usually after you have made the rounds and have exhausted your type or been exhausted by them!

Personal Confession

I will not react to women based on what my flesh feels. I will exercise discernment, using my head along with the counsel of God, when it comes to matters of the heart and choosing my mate.

A good woman is a Gleaner or a Secret Star who loves you and releases you to be the man you were created to be. When you meet this kind of woman, grab her and do not let her go. Be intentional. Make your heart known to her and ask if she would allow you to ask her parents for her hand in marriage. It is crucial that you get a blessing from both families before you marry.

In Ghana, West Africa, I love the tradition of the engagement before the wedding. It is a very serious matter, though I am giving you the abbreviated, modern version. The groom has to make an appointment with the family of the bride to come and ask for her hand. It is referred to as "the knocking." On the appropriate day, the groom, along with significant members of his family, goes to the family home of the bride bearing gifts, and formally asks for her hand. If it is granted, they proceed to make a day when "the engagement" will be made official. The day of the engagement can be as intricately planned as the wedding itself. Both sets of family gather. The older members of the family usually officiate the engagement. They tell stories and exchange banter about the two who have decided to marry. They give instruction to the couple on how to care for one another. The groom presents gifts to the family and asks formal permission from her immediate family to marry her. The father, mother, brothers, everyone must agree. He then presents the ring to her, and a major celebration with food and drink seals the engagement. It is a public declaration of their intent to become husband and wife.

Their word on that day is taken so seriously that they are considered married, even though the wedding ceremony has not taken place. In order to break the engagement, another family meeting would have to be held. The entire family would be involved, and the couple would be held accountable to the elders for their decision. It would not be easy to get out of the engagement. The couple would be urged to work out their differences before permission to go their separate ways would be granted.

Potential Blessing

Today, we have no understanding of the value of the blessing. Yet, that blessing from family sets the tone of your marriage. It places you under the umbrella of their authority and God's grace. It holds both parties accountable to their vows. It would serve us well in this country to imitate this practice. The solemnity of the promises you make to one another is fully realized. But even better is the covering it provides for a woman. How can you apply this tradition to your situation? Get the blessing. I believe it does a man good to have to ask a woman's family for permission to marry her. It keeps you rooted in the reality that what you are about to do is serious and you will be held accountable. It is important for both of you to get the families' blessing. This step is crucial.

After Boaz made his intentions clear before the elders at the gate, they not only witnessed the transaction between Boaz and his kinsman in regard to Ruth, they also declared a blessing over Boaz and his future wife. For every man I have ministered to who has been on the verge of divorce or is divorced, the same words have been repeated when I asked him how his parents felt about his spouse. "Oh, they didn't like her. They didn't want me to marry her." The parents might have gone along with the wedding plans to keep the peace, but they most certainly did not give their blessing. The absence of that blessing might as well have been a curse. It usually foretells of problems to come.

I think of the story of Samson found in Judges chapter 14. He goes off and meets a girl, then announces her as his choice to wed, completely shirking the tradition of the bridegroom's father selecting the bride for his son. Samson boldly selected his own bride against his parents wishes, then pushed them to make all the arrangements and accept his choice. Well, the rest is history. Shortly after the marriage, his bride betrayed him, and he went off in a murderous rage, making quite a few enemies. Shortly after he calmed down, he went to retrieve his bride from her father's house, only to find out she had been given to his best man! Well, he cannot say his parents did not warn him, that is for sure. I am certain they did not foresee all the coming turmoil. All they knew was that they did not feel this woman was the right one for him. Call it a parent sense or third sense if you will, but I believe that God gives parents a special sensitivity to the needs of their children, whether the parents are believers or not.

I think back to my own college sweetheart whom both of my fathers, Mr. McKinney and Mr. Hammond, resoundingly, hands down, voted out of my life. Oh, how I cried and railed. I was caught up in a modern-day Romeo and Juliet story! Every time I went through another failed relationship, I would think back to my old flame who loved the ground I walked on and say to myself that I could have been married by now if it was not for my fathers. And, of course, my mother was in agreement with them. Well, I can tell you now that they were absolutely right. At an age where I could not see the character of my beloved, my fathers could. Today that man I wanted to marry so badly is in jail for murdering a man. He beat him to death in a rage. That is who I would have been married to!

Whether you like it or not, parents have radar on these sorts of things. Their eyes are not glazed over with a delicate shade of rose as they look over your potential mate. Because they love you and know you, they are able to make discerning and objective observances of the person you present to them. Embrace the idea that God has placed parents in our lives to keep us safe—in some instances, to save us from ourselves and our sometimes impetuous, foolish choices.

You might feel you are an adult, you are grown, and you have been on your own for a long time; therefore, your parents should not have any say-so over your life. The Scripture verse that urges us to honor our father and our mother, with the promise that if we do we will have a long life and good success, rings true and has been proven so. Honoring includes considering their words, not just being nice to them. Honor has to do with obedience. No matter what age you are, they are still your parents and have the right to speak into your life. No matter how you feel, I urge you to be careful. Do not go down the aisle without that blessing! This is the greatest gift a parent can give you on your wedding day because God will honor the prayers and words of your parents.

Let me interject here that God honors the words and prayers of parents who honor their children. God answers prayers and heeds confessions He agrees with, not those spoken with a mean spirit or evil motive. I sadly realize that not everyone has had a picture-perfect family life. Some people have been abused emotionally and physically by their fathers and mothers. In this case, your parents might not be the ones to give you the blessing. Seek it from someone grounded in wisdom whom God can use as a spiritual parent to you. It might be your pastor or a godly couple in your life.

I cannot stress enough how important it is to submit your intentions to a group of people you love and trust, and really absorb their counsel. This is your safety net. If you are hesitant about this, that should let you know there is something you do not want to hear. Heed the Word of God and the words of those He has placed in your life to counsel you. It literally could be a matter of life and death—the life or death of your joy, peace, and every romantic dream you ever had of your future. Take the time for marriage counseling and get a release from your pastor and your own spirit to proceed forward. If you do your home-work before the wedding, your marriage will have a greater chance of being fruitful, joyful, and victorious.

As mature and self-made as Boaz was, even he needed the blessing and accepted it graciously. He saw it as a covering that would keep his relationship with Ruth safe. On the wings of that blessing, he moved forward to secure her hand in marriage, and we are still hearing about this incredible love story today. With the blessing in place, your marriage becomes fertile ground for bearing fruit that will serve as a testimony to other people of the faithfulness of God. In a world where people cry out to see good examples of marriage that renew their faith in true love, you can be a blessing and a beacon to those you know and love.

The Facts on Women

➤ Women work off of what you do not know when they are the wrong type of woman. Make sure you expose the woman in your life to other women you trust for counsel.

➤ A woman's approach to you will foretell how the rest of the relationship will go.

➤ It has been said that most men marry their mothers. Be honest in your assessment of the woman you are seeing and why you feel she is the one for you.

➤ A woman who truly loves you considers your happiness before her own. A self-consumed woman has her own agenda.

➤ A woman with issues will always be on the defensive and be thin-skinned when disagreed with or confronted.

➤ Wise, mature women graciously receive counsel and correction.

Consider This

- Consider the woman who is your potential mate. What characteristics about her do you treasure most?

- What concerns you about her and your relationship? How can these habits affect your marriage? Are these things you could live with if they never changed?

- If not presently dating, which type of woman have you continually dated over and over in the past? How can you break the cycle? How has this hindered you from finding true happiness?

- What people in your life would you consider important enough to get a blessing from?

◄►

*Where no counsel is, the people fall:
but in the multitude of counselors there is safety*
(Proverbs 11:14 KJV).

12
The End of the Matter

*So Boaz took Ruth and she became his wife;
and when he went in to her, the LORD gave
her conception, and she bore a son.*

RUTH 4:13 NKJV

*W*hat a beautiful picture of completion Boaz and Ruth
paint with their happy ending. Here is a couple who did it the
right way. There is something to be said for that. What starts off
right, in most cases, finishes right. What starts off wrong, well…
usually never gets right. It just gets worse. Not that I want to
mess up a good love story, but I want you to not just be married.
I want you to be married to reality as well. Just because they did
everything right at the start of the marriage does not mean that
every day was bliss. I am sure they had lots of adjustments to
make. Boaz had been single for quite a while. Ruth had been
married before and had her own way of doing things. Both of
them had to work toward becoming one, as any couple does.

I want you to be equipped to stay on your journey, even after
you have finally found your Ruth. There are a few things that you
need to consider before you start jumping up and down because
you finally "caught the fish." Once you catch a fish, that is when
the real work begins. You have to clean it and prepare it to be

edible. The same goes for marriage. However, most people are so busy gazing through rose-colored lenses that they are shocked when the real work begins. This would be the work of clearing your mind of preconceived notions of what your marriage is *supposed* to look like. You are no longer single. Now the journey begins of becoming one. Both of you will be bringing ideas and habits to the marriage that the other person did not expect. This is where things can go wrong quickly if you do not have some foundational plans under your belt.

In today's world of prenuptial agreements and no-fault divorce, the true meaning of marriage has been lost. It has been reduced to a "well, let's see if this works" format—a loveless contract. Whatever happened to those famous words that Ruth uttered to her mother-in-law, that I am sure she repeated to her new husband, Boaz? "Don't urge me to leave you....Where you go I will go....Your people will be my people and your God my God" (Ruth 1:16). Ruth understood the meaning of covenant, and so did Boaz.

You see, contracts can be broken. Every contract comes laden with loopholes. These are to protect the interest of the person who is making the agreement in case the other party does not live up to the standards of the contract. A contract is usually for a specified term and has agreed-upon requirements. If any of the specifics are not carried out, the deal is off because the interest of one person was not met. A lot of marriages are like that. Two people stand at the altar in the presence of witnesses and promise to love one another for richer for poorer, in sickness and in health, 'til death parts them, but then promptly forget their promise the first time a major trial hits. They both retreat to their own corner to ponder which of their needs are not being met by the other partner. Accusations fly. They come to the conclusion they have irreconcilable differences, and the contract is broken. Herein lies the problem. Marriage is not a contract. It is a covenant.

The Power of a Covenant

A covenant is different from a contract. There are no specified terms or expiration dates. It is forever and ever, amen. When God made a covenant with Abraham, He sealed it by appearing to him as a flaming torch passing between the split carcass of a dead animal. This was to signify the covenant was sealed in blood. This meant that one of them would have to die in order for the covenant to no longer be in effect. In the mind of God, even death does not alter a covenant. He made a covenant with David, king of Israel, that the throne would never be taken from his family lineage. Even though David messed up badly and eventually died, God honored His covenant by continuing to place David's descendants on the throne, right down to Jesus Himself!

Personal Confession

I will choose to honor the commitment I made before God and my mate. I will work through issues until a place of compromise and agreement can be made and embrace these adjustments that will take me to the next level of victorious living.

When we make a covenant at the altar by saying the profound words "'til death do us part," God expects us to honor our vow. Otherwise, we destroy everything we have worked for. According to His Word, "As iron sharpens iron, a friend sharpens a friend" (Proverbs 27:17 NLT). This has to be true of the marriage covenant.

Perhaps this is where the ball gets dropped. Because we do not have a true understanding of a covenant and the purpose of marriage, we balk at the first sign of a part of ourselves dying. But something has to die in each partner in order for them to become one. We must agree to lay down individual rights in order to grasp the greater good. Oneness empowers us to get further in life than we would individually.

What I Am Saying

Recently, I was on a radio interview discussing my book *In Search of the Proverbs 31 Man*. A listener called in and was still disturbed by the guests before me who had written a book called *The Best Thing I Ever Did for My Marriage*. The premise of their book (from what I was able to glean from the interviewer and caller) was what a woman could do for her man in order to make their marriage better. The caller was upset because she felt the authors were saying that all the work in the relationship was on the woman. She wanted to know, "What about the men? Don't they have to do anything?" She then went on into deeper, more dangerous waters by saying that in today's *new* Christianity, people should be able to be independent in a marriage and still get along!

My first reaction was that I did not know there *was* a new Christianity. I had not gotten the memo. No one had informed me that God had changed His mind on anything He had written, or changed His Word in any way. I cited that God is the same yesterday, today, and forever. Therefore, His rules on marriage have not changed. The bottom line is that both people, man and woman, are called to submit to one another. The man's assignment is clear: to protect, provide for, love, and cherish his woman. The woman is still called to submit to, respect, and serve her husband. This is something she will do naturally if the man is doing his job.

If he is *not* doing his job, she should continue doing the right thing anyway, and vice versa. Two wrongs do not make a right. The lifestyle of both partners versus their demands will make a change in each other because God will honor them for staying in the right place. I know that might sound too simple, and sometimes the condition of a marriage is far more complicated. However, no one should cause you to sin. We are called to do all that we do as unto the Lord, knowing in the end God is the One we will answer to. If the man does not treat his wife as he should, God will deal with him in His own way. We do not hear a lot preached on this, but God is serious about men treating women properly. As a matter of fact, if they don't, it could cost them answered prayer!

A covenant says you keep your end of the bargain no matter what. God kept His end of the deal with David in spite of his failings. David, however, was not exempt from suffering the consequences of his actions. When he entered into an adulterous relationship, he suffered severe losses for it. The chain reaction from sin is frightening. The Bible says the adulterer is reduced to a loaf of bread (Proverbs 6:26), and another man will eat his inheritance (Proverbs 5:10). God will not be mocked. Though forgiven, we still bear the scars of our sin.

What I am saying is that, for the most part, we have cultivated an independent society that grows more selfish by the decade. *What about what I want? What about what I need?* This attitude cannot be carried into a covenant relationship. A covenant relationship is based on give-and-give, on dying and dying again, until all that stands between the two of you has passed away. It is no longer *I,* but *we.* I can always tell where a relationship stands between two people by the language they use. I can tell which partner is having a struggle, not just by body language—who leans in and who leans away—but also by their words. One will say, "*We* are going to do this." The other will say "*I* am going to do this."

When we come into covenant with God, we are called to die daily, to take up our cross and walk, to sacrifice the urgency of our flesh for the call of the Spirit. The closer we draw to God while laying aside anything that stands in the way of our relationship with Him, the more blessed we become. We become more free to experience the life we want after all—filled with righteousness, peace, and joy in the Holy Ghost. The peace that passes all understanding fills us to overflowing because we have finally gotten ourselves out of the way. The same is true in our physical relationships.

How is this achieved? It is done by getting the focus off ourselves and truly seeking to know the other person. What are her needs, her desires, the things that move her heart and make her feel loved and secure? We will discover our own needs being met as we pour out our lives to that other person. The natural response for the other person is to give back because there is no room for her to consider what she lacks. A breakdown happens when your wife tries to fill on her own the needs she feels you are ignoring. Do not give her the room to go there. When she is satisfied, she will seek to satisfy you. This applies to every level of the relationship—from conversation, to daily interaction, to the intimacy of the marriage bed. Remember, foreplay starts at the beginning of the day, not before you go to bed. If you learn to practice romance in your marriage, the honeymoon can be relived again and again.

The story tells us that Boaz took Ruth to be his wife. In the King James version it says that Boaz "knew" her, and she conceived and bore a son. As a couple takes the time to truly know one another and unselfishly fill one another's needs, their marriage will bear fruit in accordance with God's timing and design, whether that be in the form of children or spiritual fruit. God chooses what will glorify Him most in the life of each couple. Most importantly, their love will continue to grow because it is being nurtured and fertilized with acts of kindness and selflessness.

As I look at couples who have been together for a long time, who have weathered the storms and worked through their differences, I get a picture of what God had in mind: oneness. They even begin to look alike. They anticipate one another's needs and finish one another's sentences. I see tender men and women who are in tune with one another. When commenting on this to these couples, they are quick to say it was not always that way. They had their struggles, but they endured.

In order to find common ground with our mates, we must be willing to move ourselves out of the way and truly hear the other person. Our love for each other should compel us to seek the other's greater good. Two people inclined toward this end bring out the best in one another and bear fruit that feeds not only them, but also people around them. It restores the faith of singles who have lost hope in the idea of marriage. It makes children feel safe when they look at their parents and see nothing but love and cooperation. This feeling of safety makes children better members of society, whole and balanced. They are able to go out into the world and have meaningful relationships, mirroring what they see at home.

The Truth About Your House

There is a prevalent attitude in our society that says, "It is nobody's business what goes on in my house." This philosophy cannot be further from the truth. What happens in your house will eventually affect other people. A divided house affects everyone in the house. When people leave the house, their attitudes can seriously affect others, sometimes to deadly proportions. God meant for a covenant to give people security and strength to go out into the world and perform at their best. They are to be infused by the love they get at home and have it be contagious at school, in the marketplace, wherever they go.

The entire concept of two people becoming one has far-reaching implications. Your oneness becomes a legacy that is left to the next generation. Two people having a relationship steeped in wholeness produces children who go on to affect society long after you have departed the earth. Ruth and Boaz had a son, who had a son, who had a son that changed the entire destiny of a nation. Not only that, but their descendant was of the lineage of Jesus Christ. The fruit we bear in our homes eventually affects the world at large, whether we will ever witness the effect or not. What type of fruit do you want to bear in your home?

The Fruit We Bear

I find it ironic that Ruth (meaning "friendship") had no children by her first husband—you know, the one named Mahlon (his name meant "sickly"). Nothing can grow in a sickly environment and become whole. Because Mahlon was sickly, their marriage bore no fruit except death. Though we all can be transformed by the power of the Spirit of God, some people never experience the breakthroughs they could because of their state of mind. Mahlon was probably used to being sickly and had accepted his fate, no longer seeking a solution or victory for his life. Attitude is everything when dealing with the issues of life. With a sickly frame of mind, he would not have the strength to rise above where he was in order to give birth to something different in his life.

This is why it is so important for a man to truly know and be cognizant of the character of a woman before he marries her. Boaz (meaning "strength") and Ruth were both made of the right stuff. Together they had what was required for bearing rich fruit. The man is called not just to be a provider and protector for the woman; he is designed to be her strength. In this most important facet of his being, she rests. A woman is called to be not only a helper for her husband; she is also called to be his friend. This is one of the greatest needs a man has from the woman in his life. These two characteristics cement them as a couple.

When friendship is joined to strength, incredible things happen. A couple has the ability to give birth to things that will leave a rich legacy—a testimony of a marriage that is a fine example for other people to aspire to and follow. Children with a heritage of sound character and integrity can make wonderful contributions to the people around them and perhaps even to the world.

And how about your own personal satisfaction? When you lay your head down at the end of the day and look at your wife, your Ruth, lying beside you, desire overwhelms you when you think of what her love has done to you as a man. As you reach to embrace her tenderly, loving her unconditionally, you are able to say quietly in your heart to God, *This woman was well worth the wait.*

 The Facts on Women

➤ A woman finds it easy to submit to a man who is submitted to God.

➤ A woman was made for a covenant. Her nature embraces it.

➤ A wounded woman will withdraw from her husband and find it hard to submit to him because her pain destroys her respect for him. Keep short accounts when it comes to offenses.

➤ Women are moved by what they hear. Use words to draw her to you. Use loving actions to keep her in your embrace.

Consider This

- What is your understanding of a covenant?

- Why do you want to be married? What do you expect to get out of it? What are you prepared to give? What are you prepared to sacrifice?

- What lasting legacy would you like your marriage to have?

◄►

For this reason a man will leave his father
and mother and be united to his wife,
and they will become one flesh (Genesis 2:24).

Other Books by Michelle McKinney Hammond

What to Do Until Love Finds You
Secrets of an Irresistible Woman
Where Are You, God?
Get a Love Life
If Men Are Like Buses, Then How Do I Catch One?
Prayer Guide for the Brokenhearted
What Becomes of the Brokenhearted?
How to Be Blessed and Highly Favored
Get Over It and On With It
Why Do I Say "Yes" When I Need to Say "No"?
Sassy, Single, and Satisfied
The Unspoken Rules of Love
In Search of the Proverbs 31 Man
101 Ways to Get and Keep His Attention
The D.I.V.A. Principle
The D.I.V.A. Principle: A Sistergirl's Guide
The Power of Being a Woman

To correspond with Michelle McKinney Hammond,
you may write to her:

c/o Heartwing Ministries
P.O. Box 11052
Chicago, IL 60611

E-mail her at heartwingmin@yahoo.com

Or log on to her website at:

www.michellehammond.com
or www.heartwing.org

For information on booking her
for a speaking engagement:

Call 1-866-391-0955 or log on to
www.michellehammond.com